GOD HAS BIG PLANS FOR YOU, ESTHER

KAY ARTHUR
JANNA ARNDT

HARVEST HOUSE PUBLISHERS
EUGENE, OREGON

All Scripture quotations in this book are taken from the New American Standard Bible®, © 1960, 1962, 1963, 1968, 1971, 1972, 1973, 1975, 1977, 1995 by The Lockman Foundation. Used by permission. (www.Lockman.org)

Illustrations © 2011 by Steve Bjorkman

Cover by Left Coast Design, Portland, Oregon

DISCOVER 4 YOURSELF is a registered trademark of The Hawkins Children's LLC. Harvest House Publishers, Inc., is the exclusive licensee of the federally registered trademark DISCOVER 4 YOURSELF.

HARVEST KIDS is a registered trademark of The Hawkins Children's LLC. Harvest House Publishers, Inc., is the exclusive licensee of the federally registered trademark HARVEST KIDS.

Certified Sourcing
www.sfiprogram.org
SFI-00453

GOD HAS BIG PLANS FOR YOU, ESTHER
Copyright © 2011 by Precept Ministries International
Published by Harvest House Publishers
Eugene, Oregon 97402
www.harvesthousepublishers.com

ISBN 978-0-7369-2596-9 (Softcover)
ISBN 978-0-7369-4127-3 (eBook)

Printed in the United States of America

17 18 19 20 21 22 23 / ML-NI / 10 9 8 7 6 5 4 3

CONTENTS

Discovering God's Plan—
A Bible Study You Can Do!

Discovering God's Plan—

A Bible Study You Can Do!

Hey, guys! Guess what? Molly, Sam (the great face-licking detective beagle), and I are headed to Washington, D.C., to visit our Uncle Matt and meet the president of the United States of America. By the way, my name is Max. Can you believe we are going to meet the president? Not only will we meet the president and learn about the United States government while we tour the nation's capital, but we'll also study the life of a young lady in the Bible whom God used to change the course of her nation. Her story is found in the book of Esther, a fascinating historical book in the Bible that shows us what happened to God's chosen people during the time of the Medes and the Persians.

As we arrive in Washington, D.C., we're going to study the most important book in history—the Bible—to find out WHO the main characters are in Esther. WHY did God put these people in the palace at this time in history? WHAT is happening? WHAT plot is uncovered? WHO will live? WHO will die? WHAT is God's purpose and plan?

You'll get the answers to all these questions by going straight to God's Word, the Bible, the source of all truth, and asking God's Spirit to lead and guide you.

You also have this book, which is an inductive Bible study. *Inductive* means you go straight to the Bible *yourself* to investigate what the book of Esther shows you about a young orphan girl God puts in a palace to bring about His plan for His people and an entire nation. In inductive Bible study you discover for yourself what the Bible says and means.

Aren't you excited? Grab your Bible and get ready for an *incredible* adventure as you discover God's perfect plan to rescue and restore His people!

THINGS YOU'LL NEED

NEW AMERICAN STANDARD BIBLE
(UPDATED EDITION)—
PREFERABLY THE NEW INDUCTIVE
STUDY BIBLE (HAVE YOU
GOTTEN YOURS YET?)

PEN OR PENCIL

COLORED PENCILS

INDEX CARDS

A DICTIONARY

THIS WORKBOOK

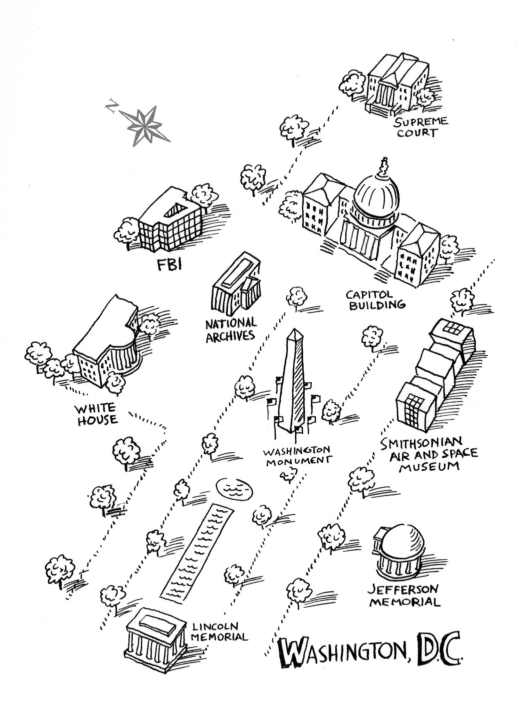

SUPREME
COURT

FBI

CAPITOL
BUILDING

NATIONAL
ARCHIVES

WHITE
HOUSE

WASHINGTON
MONUMENT

SMITHSONIAN
AIR AND SPACE
MUSEUM

JEFFERSON
MEMORIAL

LINCOLN
MEMORIAL

WASHINGTON, D.C.

1

A ROYAL BANQUET

ESTHER 1

"We are so glad you're here! Molly and I are excited to have you with us on our new adventure in Washington, D.C., with our Uncle Matt. Do you remember Uncle Matt from our special mission in the Discover 4 Yourself Bible study *God, What's Your Name?* Uncle Matt is a secret agent for the CIA, but this time his mission is to show us around our nation's capital as we study the book of Esther to see how God uses His people to change the course of a nation.

"This is going to be so cool! Uncle Matt has also gotten us a very special invitation to meet the president of the United States so we can get a firsthand glimpse at being the leader of a nation.

"Are you ready to get started on this awesome adventure? Then grab the most important book in history—the Bible—and let's find out WHO the main characters are in Esther as we make our first stop in D.C."

RESEARCH

"Hi, kids!" Uncle Matt hugged Max and Molly as Sam watched for the perfect moment to jump up and give Uncle Matt a good face-licking. "Uh, you got me, Sam! I should have known better than to take my eyes off you even for a moment."

"Hey, he's a better secret agent than you!" Max teased, as Molly and Uncle Matt laughed and Sam wagged his tail.

"We're here," Uncle Matt announced as he led the kids into the National Archives building. "The National Archives is the nation's record keeper. It is where the United States keeps all the documents and materials that record important events in American history. This is also where copies of the Charters of Freedom are kept."

"What are the Charters of Freedom, Uncle Matt?" Molly asked.

"The Charters of Freedom are three very important documents in American history concerning the founding of our country," Uncle Matt replied.

"Oh, I bet I know what those three documents are," Max said, jumping into the conversation. "The Declaration of Independence, the Constitution, and the Bill of Rights."

"You're right, Max," Uncle Matt answered. "Before we head into the rotunda to get a close-up look at these important documents, let's go into the research room to start our investigation of Esther. Now that we're here, WHAT is the first thing we need to do before we get started?"

"Pray!" Max and Molly said at the same time. Sam barked in agreement.

"That's right!" Uncle Matt smiled at their answer. "Bible study should always begin with prayer. We need to ask God to help us understand what the Bible says and to direct us by His Holy Spirit so we can make sure we understand His Word and handle it accurately. Let's talk to God."

All right! Now that we have prayed, let's get to work on our research. Did you know that Esther is a historical book in the Bible? Since you study history in school, you know that history is about people and events in the past.

Today we need to find the historical setting and the main characters in the book of Esther by using Observation Worksheets. Observation Worksheets have the Bible text printed out for us so we can study the book of Esther.

To discover the setting and characters of Esther, we need to ask the 5 W's and an H. What are the 5 W's and an H? They are the WHO, WHAT, WHERE, WHEN, WHY, and HOW questions.

1. Since this book is a historical book, asking WHO is very important. Asking WHO helps you find out:

   WHO are the main characters?

   WHO is involved?

   WHO said this or did that?

2. WHAT helps you understand:

   WHAT are the main events taking place?

   WHAT is God telling you?

3. WHEN tells us about time. We mark it with a green clock or a green circle like this: ◯ . WHEN tells us:

   WHEN did this event happen or WHEN is it going to happen?

   WHEN is so very important in history. It helps us follow the order of events.

4. In any historical event, WHERE is very important. WHERE helps you learn:

   WHERE did something happen?

   WHERE did the people go?

WHERE was something said?

When we discover a "WHERE," we double-underline the "WHERE" in green.

5. Looking at history, WHY asks questions like:

   WHY did this event happen?

   WHY did the people say that?

   WHY did they go there?

6. HOW lets you figure out things like:

   HOW did something happen?

   HOW did the people react to what happened?

Now that you know what the 5W's and an H are, turn to page 160. Read Esther 1:1-9 on your Observation Worksheet. Then ask those 5 W's and an H questions.

Esther 1:1 WHEN does Esther take place?

In the days of ___Ahaserus___.

Draw a green clock 🕐 or a green circle ◯ over this time phrase in Esther 1:1 on page 160.

Esther 1:1-9 WHO are the main characters?

King ___Ahaserus___ and Queen ___Vashti___

Esther 1:1 WHERE did Ahasuerus rule?

From ___India___ to ___Ethiopia___ over ___127___ provinces

Esther 1:2 WHERE was Ahasuerus's royal throne?

At the ___citadel___ in ___Susa___

Double-underline the WHERE in Esther 1:1-2 in green on page 160. Then look at the following map and double-underline the location of Ahasuerus's royal throne.

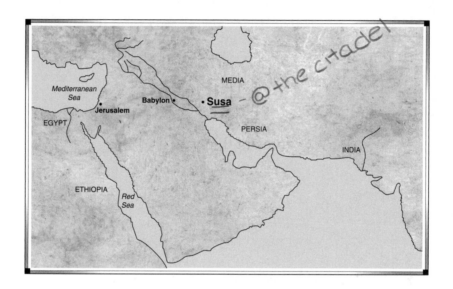

Esther 1:3 WHEN in Ahasuerus's reign is this happening?

In the ___third___ year of his reign

Draw a green clock 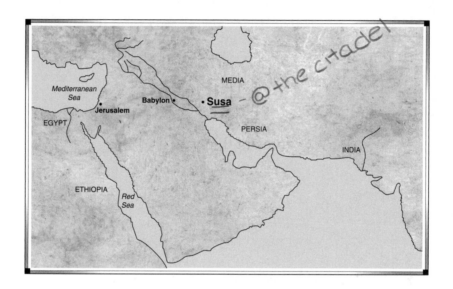 or a green circle ◯ over this time phrase on page 160.

Esther 1:3 WHAT kingdom is ruling at this time in history?

The kingdom of P e r s i a and M e d i a

Great work! You have done some awesome research! You just discovered the setting for the book of Esther. You went straight to God's Word, the Book of truth, and saw that Esther takes place during the kingdom of the Medes and the Persians. You also saw that it is the third year of the reign of a king named Ahasuerus, and that he has a wife named Queen Vashti. Tomorrow, as you continue your research, you will find out more about Persian King Ahasuerus and his wife, Queen Vashti.

Before you wrap up your research today, you have one more thing to discover: your memory verse. Each week in our study, you will learn a new memory verse. In order to know God, you need to know His Word and have it hidden in your heart.

Discover this week's memory verse by looking at the following book. Unscramble the words underneath the blanks in the book, and put the correct word on each blank. Find the reference for this verse in Esther 1 and write it in.

Then get an index card and write this verse on your card. Practice saying it out loud three times in a row, three times today!

"For the queen's conduct will become known
                   onctduc   nowkn

to all the women causing them to look with contempt
          omwen   onctepmt

on their husbands by saying, 'King Ahaserus
         ushsbdan   hasAruseu

commanded Queen Vashti to be brought in to
omcadmned   aVhtsi

his presence, but she did not come.'"
    respceen   omce

Esther 1:17

You did it! We are so proud of you! Now head to the rotunda and take a look at the Charters of Freedom that established the United States.

DAY TWO

A LOOK AT THE KING

"Wow! This is incredible!" Max exclaimed. "I can't believe we are standing in the National Archives building looking at the Declaration of Independence. Can you believe we are looking at the document that announced the independence of the United States of America from Great Britain on July 4, 1776?"

"It's amazing," Molly agreed. "Listen to this part: 'We hold these truths to be self-evident, that all men are created equal, that they are endowed by their Creator with certain unalienable Rights, that among these are Life, Liberty, and the pursuit of Happiness.'"

"Did you know that sentence has been called one of the best-known sentences in the English language?" Uncle Matt asked. "The Declaration of Independence was written to secure the people's rights and to state that when a government doesn't honor those rights, then it is the right of the people to alter the government or get it abolished for their safety."

"That's so cool to see how our Founding Fathers wanted to make sure the government worked for the people," Molly added.

"You're right, Molly!" responded Uncle Matt. "Now that we've seen the Declaration of Independence, let's head back into the research room to find out what is happening in Esther by reading the Bible!"

Yesterday we discovered two main characters: a king named Ahasuerus and a queen named Vashti. Today we need to get the details on one of our main characters. One way we can uncover clues about main characters is to color-code their names in a special way in the Bible so we can get a clearer look at them. Today we are going to read all of Esther 1 and color every place we see the name *Ahasuerus* orange. When you color *Ahasuerus*, you will also need to color any other words that mean the same thing, such as pronouns and synonyms. What are pronouns?

Pronouns

Pronouns are words that take the place of nouns. A noun is a person, place, or thing. A pronoun stands in for a noun. Look at the two sentences below. Watch how the pronoun *he* is substituted for Max's name in the second sentence.

> "*Max* can't wait to meet the president of the United States. *He* hopes the president will invite him into the Oval Office."

The word *he* is a pronoun because it takes the place of Max's name in the second sentence. *He* is another word we use to refer to Max.

Watch for these pronouns when you are marking people's names:

I	you	he	she
me	yours	him	her
mine		his	hers
we	it		
our	its		
they	them		

Now take a look at the next box to learn about synonyms.

Synonyms

Synonyms are different words that mean the same thing. In Esther 1, *king* is another word for *Ahasuerus* and *queen* is another word for *Vashti*. That's a synonym. It says the same thing but with a different word.

Now that you know what pronouns and synonyms are, turn to your Observation Worksheets on page 160. Read Esther 1 and color every reference to Ahasuerus in a special way, just like this:

Ahasuerus (King Ahasuerus, king) (color it orange)

All right! Now that we have marked our Observation Worksheet, let's find out WHAT we can learn about King Ahasuerus from each of these verses. Look at every place where you marked a reference to King Ahasuerus by coloring it orange on your Observation Worksheet. Make a list of everything you learned about him.

My List on King Ahasuerus

Esther 1:1 King Ahasuerus reigned from _India_ to _Ethopia_ over _127_ provinces.

Esther 1:2 King Ahasuerus's royal throne was at the _citadel_ in _Susa_.

Esther 1:3 In the _third_ year of Ahasuerus's _reign_, he gave a _banquet_ for

all his _princes_ and _attendants_, the
Army officers of Persia and Media,
the _nobles_ and the _princes_ of his
provinces.

Esther 1:4 King Ahasuerus displayed the _riches_
of his _royal glory_ and the _splendor_
of his great _majesty_ for _180_ days.

Esther 1:5 King Ahasuerus gave another _banquet_
that lasted _7_ days for all the _people_ who
were present at the citadel in _Susa_ in the
court of the _garden_ of the king's
palace.

Esther 1:8 The king gave _orders_ to each
official of his household that he should do according to the desires of each person.

Esther 1:10-11 King Ahasuerus was _merry_
with wine and commanded the seven eunuchs
to bring _Queen Vashti_ before him to
display her _beauty_ to the _people_
and the _princes_.

Esther 1:12 The king became very _angry_ and
his _wrath_ burned within him.

Esther 1:13-15 King Ahasuerus spoke to the wise men about what to do with Queen Vashti since she did not obey.

Esther 1:17 King Ahasuerus commanded Queen Vashti to be brought in to his presence.

Esther 1:20 The king will make his edict heard throughout his kingdom.

Esther 1:21 King Ahasuerus was p l e a s ed with the word and did as Memucan proposed.

Fantastic! Just look at all we learned about this king! King Ahasuerus is the king over a great empire, the kingdom of Persia and Media. He is a very wealthy king, who gives two different banquets, according to Esther 1. Historians think King Ahasuerus gave these banquets and invited his army officers so they could plan his invasion of Greece.

We also see that King Ahasuerus loves beautiful things and takes great pride in what he has. He wants all the people to see the riches and splendor that belong to him. And King Ahasuerus is also a king who gets very angry when Queen Vashti, his beautiful wife, refuses to come to his banquet.

Uh-oh! WHAT will this angry king do? We'll find out as we continue to do our research. Don't forget to practice your memory verse. Say it out loud three times in a row, three times today!

DAY THREE

RESEARCH ON THE QUEEN

"I just love working in the National Archives building, Uncle Matt," Molly said as they headed back into the research room.

"Yeah," Max added. "It's pretty cool doing our research in here with all these pieces of American history around us. We can look at the Constitution of the United States and think about how the Founding Fathers of our nation wrote the Constitution because they wanted to form a government that did not allow one person to have too much authority or control. They saw how bad that could be while they were under the rule of the British king."

Uncle Matt asked Molly, "What is the Constitution?"

"The Constitution is a set of rules for us to live by, that also provides a separation of powers so that one person won't have too much control. That's why there are three separate branches of our government."

"That's right, Molly," Uncle Matt agreed. "Each branch of the United States government works together to make our country run smoothly and to make sure the rights of Americans are protected."

Max smiled. "That's called checks and balances. One branch of the government can use its power to check the powers of the other two branches to keep the power balanced among all three branches."

"You've got it, Max. Okay, Molly, what are the three branches of government?"

"The legislative, executive, and judicial."

"Great work, kids!"

Okay, you guys, now that we have taken a look at our Constitution, we need to get back to our research in Esther to find out more about what is happening in the times of the Medes and Persians. WHAT can we learn about the queen in Esther 1? Don't forget to talk to your King before you get started!

All right! Now that you have prayed, turn to your Observation Worksheet on page 160. Read Esther 1 and mark every reference to Vashti in a special way, just like we have:

Vashti (Queen Vashti, queen) (color it green)

Don't forget to mark the pronouns!

Awesome! Now let's see what we can learn about Queen Vashti. Look at every place where you colored a reference to Queen Vashti green in Esther 1 and make a list of what you discovered about her.

My List on Queen Vashti

Esther 1:9 Queen Vashti gave a _banquet_ for the _women_ in the palace.

Esther 1:11 Queen Vashti was commanded to come before the _king_ with her royal _crown_ to display her _beauty_ to the _people_ and the ___princes___. Queen Vashti was ___beautiful___.

Esther 1:12 Queen Vashti ___refused___ to ___come___ at the king's command.

Esther 1:15 Queen Vashti did not ___obey___ the ___command___ of King Ahasuerus.

Esther 1:16 Queen Vashti w ___r o n g___ ed the ___king___ and all the ___princes___ and all the ___people___ who are in all the provinces of King Ahasuerus.

Esther 1:17 Queen Vashti's ___conduct___ will become known to all the ___women___. She was ___commanded___ by King Ahasuerus to be brought into his presence but she did not ___come___.

Amazing! Can you believe Queen Vashti refused to honor the king and come into his presence? She didn't obey the king's command.

How about you? How do you respond to those in authority over you? Do you obey your parents like the Bible says you should in Ephesians 6:1-3?

_____ Yes   _____ No   _X_ Sometimes

Do you obey those in authority over you like it says to in Romans 13:1?

_____ Yes   _____ No   _X_ Sometimes

How do you talk to your parents and teachers? Do you speak to them with respect? Or does your tone of voice show disrespect, anger, or impatience? Write down how you treat your parents and teachers when they correct you or ask you to do something.

I treat my parents w/ disrespect, I need to fix that.

Vashti is a queen. She is a leader and role model for the people in her country.

Esther 1:17 Looking at Queen Vashti's behavior and example, WHAT is the concern about how the other women in that country will treat their husbands?

that they will do the same thing

According to Esther 1:17, WHAT kind of leader is Queen Vashti to the women in her kingdom?

she is an arrogant leader to all women

Think about what you have learned today. Are you a good example to your brothers or sisters? *sometimes*

How about to your friends and the other kids at school? *yes*

How about to your teachers? *yes*

Write out a way you can be a good example to people—to show them by the way you behave that Jesus lives in you.

be respectful, kind, nice, ect. do things that honor God.

Way to go! Don't forget to practice your memory verse. Be a good role model for the kids who are watching you!

DAY FOUR

A ROYAL INVITATION

"Okay, guys," Uncle Matt said as they walked inside the building, "today's our last day at the archives, so let's take a look at the last of the three documents of the Charters of Freedom—the Bill of Rights."

Holding Sam, Max walked up to the Bill of Rights to take a closer look. "When the Constitution was written, some people didn't want to approve the document because it didn't have a list of rights that belonged to the people."

"Good," Uncle Matt said and smiled. "So how did they make a way to add a list of rights for the people, Molly?"

"By making an amendment process. An amendment is a change that can be added to the Constitution or it can change an older part of the Constitution. The new government held meetings, and Congress proposed a list of rights for the people. And in 1791, ten of those changes were agreed to by the states and added to the Constitution."

"Those changes," Max added, "are called the Bill of Rights, and they were written to protect the people's rights, including freedom of speech, freedom of the press, freedom of religion, the right to assemble peaceably, and many others."

"Great work, you two. It's important to understand these three historical documents because they give us our freedom as Americans.

"Let's take a moment to thank God for these freedoms He has given us as a nation and ask for His help as we continue our study on the book of Esther. Today we're going to find out WHAT the main event is in Esther 1."

All right! Now that we've talked to God, let's continue our research by marking key words. What are *key words?* Key words are words that pop up more than once. They are called key words because they help unlock the meaning of the chapter or book that you are studying and give you clues about what is most important in a passage of Scripture.

Key Words

✓ Key words are usually used over and over again. (That's because God doesn't want you to miss the point.)

✓ Key words are important.

✓ Key words are used by the writer for a reason.

Once you discover a key word, you need to mark it in a special way using a special color or symbol so you can immediately spot it in Scripture.

You may also want to make a bookmark for these key words so that you can see them at a glance as you mark them on your Observation Worksheets.

To make a key-word bookmark, get an index card or a piece of paper and write on it the key words, as well as how you are going to mark them on your Observation Worksheets.

Now turn to page 160. Read Esther 1 and mark the following key words on your Observation Worksheet:

   (banquet) (circle it in brown)

   angry (color it red)

   edict (royal edict) (box it in purple)

Don't forget to mark the pronouns! And mark anything that tells you WHERE by double-underlining the WHERE in green. Mark anything that tells you WHEN by drawing a green clock 🕐 or green circle like this: ○ .

WHAT is the main event in Esther 1? Read Esther 1:3, 5, and 9. WHAT key word shows us the main event that is happening in these verses? __banquet__

HOW many banquets are there in Esther 1? __3__

Banquet #1

Esther 1:3 WHO gives the first banquet?

__King Ahaseurhus__

Esther 1:3 WHOM did the king invite?

His __princes__ and __attendants__,

the __army officers__

of Persia and Media, the _nobles_ and the _princes_ of his provinces

Esther 1:4 HOW long did this banquet last?

180 days

Esther 1:4 WHAT happens at this banquet? WHAT did the king display?

his royal glory and riches

Banquet #2

Esther 1:5 WHO gives the second banquet?

King Anaseurus

Esther 1:5 HOW long did this banquet last?

7 days

Esther 1:5 WHO was invited to this banquet?

people present in Susa

Esther 1:5 WHERE was this banquet held?

In the _court_ of the _garden_ of the _king's palace_

Esther 1:6-8 WHAT is this banquet like?

There were _hangings_ of fine _white_

and _violet linen_, held by _cords_ of
fine _purple_ linen on _silver rings_
and _marble columns_, and _couches_
of _gold_ and _silver_ on a mosaic
pavement of _porphyry_, _marble_,
mother-of-_pearl_ and _precious_
stones.

Drinks were served in _golden_ vessels of
various kinds, and the royal _wine_ was
plentiful according to the king's bounty.

The drinking was done according to the _law_.

Esther 1:10-11 WHAT happens on the seventh day of
this banquet?

The king wants to show-off the queen's beauty.

Banquet #3

Esther 1:9 WHO gives the third banquet?

Queen Vashti

Esther 1:9 WHO is invited to this banquet?

all the women

> *Esther 1:9* WHERE is this banquet held?
>
> In the _palace_ which belonged to _king Ahaseurus_

Wow! You have just seen three incredible banquets. Tomorrow we will get the details on what happens when the king commands the queen to come to his banquet. Don't forget to practice your memory verse!

THE KiNG'S EDiCT

"We love Washington, D.C., Uncle Matt," Max said as they ate lunch outside at the National Mall. "Look at all we have learned so far just from visiting the National Archives."

Uncle Matt smiled. "Just wait, you two. There is some pretty great stuff coming up."

Sam barked as he jumped out of Max's lap and landed on Uncle Matt's lap.

"Yes, you too, Sam! I have something exciting for you too!"

Max and Molly laughed as Uncle Matt patted Sam and Sam wagged his tail.

"Let's finish up our lunch so we can get back to our study on Esther. We need to get the details on what happens at the king's second banquet when he asks the queen to come."

Talk to God. Then turn to page 160. Read Esther 1. Ask the 5 W's and an H questions to find out what happens next.

Esther 1:11 WHY did the king want the queen to come to his banquet?

To display her beauty to the people and the princes

Esther 1:12 HOW does Queen Vashti respond?

She refused to come at the king's command.

Esther 1:12 HOW did the king respond?

The king became very angry and his wrath burned within him.

Esther 1:13 WHOM did the king ask for help?

The wise men

Esther 1:15 WHAT question was asked?

"According to the law, what is to be done with Queen Vashti, because she did not obey the command of King Ahasuerus?"

Esther 1:16 WHAT did Queen Vashti do?

She wronged the king, the princes, and all the people who lived in the provinces of King Ahasuerus.

Esther 1:17 HOW did Memucan believe the women of the kingdom would respond to the queen's conduct?

They would look with contempt on their husbands.

Esther 1:19 WHAT is the solution the wise men came up with?

"Let a royal edict be issued by the king."

Esther 1:19 WHAT did we learn about the laws of Persia and Media?

They cannot be repealed .

Esther 1:19 WHAT is this royal edict?

That Vashti may no longer come into the presence of King Ahasuerus, and that her royal position will be given to another who is more worthy than she.

Esther 1:20 WHAT does Memucan say the king's edict will cause the women to do when it is heard throughout the kingdom?

All women will give honor to their husbands.

Esther 1:21 HOW did the king respond?

He was pleased and did as Memucan proposed.

Esther 1:22 WHAT did the letters say that were sent to all the king's provinces?

"That every man should be the master in his own house and the one who speaks in the language of his own people."

Look at the word search. Find each word from the blanks in the questions on pages 30-31 and circle them. If a word is used more than once, you only have to find and circle it one time.

D	E	P	M	V	M	E	T	P	H	P	W
E	N	E	R	A	A	P	S	U	F	O	O
G	N	A	S	E	M	S	S	I	D	S	R
N	H	T	M	E	S	B	H	E	W	I	T
O	E	T	T	M	A	E	S	T	T	T	H
R	H	N	A	N	O	A	N	C	I	I	Y
W	O	C	D	R	E	C	I	C	W	O	L
C	N	S	G	L	W	D	O	N	E	N	A
L	O	I	P	B	E	A	U	T	Y	A	Y
W	R	R	E	P	E	A	L	E	D	M	O
Y	R	G	N	A	D	E	S	U	F	E	R
W	O	B	E	Y	K	E	S	U	O	H	N

Are you surprised at the king's decision to remove Queen Vashti? WHAT will happen after the king banishes his queen? We'll find out as we discover two new people who are very important in this part of God's history.

Find a grown-up and say your memory verse out loud. Ask that person how you can be a good example to others.

Way to go! We are so proud of you!

2

A NEW QUEEN

ESTHER 2

Hi, guys! Today we are going to Capitol Hill to learn about Congress as we continue our research in the book of Esther.

Last week, as we opened up the most important book in history—the Bible, we saw a Persian king named Ahasuerus give two banquets to show off all his riches and witnessed Queen Vashti refusing to come at his command. The king was so angry that he goes to his wise men for help, and a royal edict is issued that Vashti will no longer be queen. What will happen next? Let's head back to Esther to find out.

DAY ONE

A LONELY KING

"Here we are!" Max cried as they stood on the steps of the Capitol building. "We are on Capitol Hill, the legislative branch of our government where laws are made."

Molly sighed. "It's so great to be here, Uncle Matt, to see in person how our government works."

"That's very important, Molly," Uncle Matt said. "When you and Max are adults, you will be among the ones to elect the leaders of our country. Three important jobs of Congress are to speak for the people, to make the laws for our country, and to oversee the executive branch of our government.

"Before we go inside to sit in the gallery to watch Congress work, let's continue our research in Esther to find out what happens now that King Ahasuerus has issued an edict that Vashti will no longer be the queen. Max, why don't you pray?"

"I sure will, Uncle Matt."

All right! Let's work on Esther 2. Turn to page 162. Read Esther 2 and mark the following key words on your Observation Worksheet. Add any new words to your key-word bookmark.

King Ahasuerus (king) (color it orange)

Vashti (color it green)

Esther (Hadassah) (color it pink)

Mordecai (color it blue)

Jew (draw a blue Star of David like this: ✡)

banquet (circle it in brown)

anger (angry) (color it red)

favor (color it yellow)

Don't forget to mark the pronouns! And mark anything that tells you WHERE by double-underlining the WHERE in green. Mark anything that tells you WHEN by drawing a green clock ⏰ or green circle like this: ◯.

Let's find out what is happening in Esther 2. Ask the 5 W's and an H.

Esther 2:1 WHOM does King Ahasuerus remember?

Ex-Queen Vashti

Esther 2:1 WHAT does King Ahasuerus remember about Vashti after his anger subsides?

what Vashti had done.

Esther 2:3 WHAT did the king's attendants suggest to the king?

"Let the king _appoint overseers_ in all the _provinces_ of his _kingdom_ that they may _gather_ every _beautiful young virgin_ to the _citadel_ of _Susa_, to the _harem_, into the _custody_ of Hegai…and let their _cosemetics_ be given them."

Esther 2:4 "Let the young lady who _pleases_ the king be _queen_ in place of _Vashti_."

Esther 2:4 HOW did King Ahasuerus feel about this idea, and WHAT did he do?

"The matter _pleased_ the king and he did _accordingly_."

Esther 2:5 WHO was at the citadel in Susa?

Mordecai

Esther 2:7 WHOM was Mordecai bringing up?

Hadassah or E-
sther

Esther 2:8 WHO was taken into the king's palace when the decree of the king was heard?

Many _young ladies_,
including _Esther_

Esther 2:9 WHO pleased Hegai? _Esther_

Esther 2:12 WHEN would each young lady go in to see the king?

At the end of her _twelve months,_
when the days of her _beautification_
were c _o m p l e t e d_

Esther 2:12 HOW long were the days of her beautification?

_____SIX_____ months with _____oils_____ of _____myrrh_____

and _____SIX_____ months with _____spices_____ and the

_____cosemetics_____ for women

Esther 2:13 HOW would the young lady go to see the king?

_____anything that she_____
_____wanted from the_____
_____palace was hers._____

Esther 2:14 WHEN would the young lady go to see the king, and WHEN would she return?

She would go to see the king in the _____evening_____

and return in the _____morning_____.

Esther 2:14 WHERE would she return to?

_____the second harem_____

Esther 2:14 Will the young lady go in again to see the king?

_____not unless summ-_____
_____oned_____

You have just discovered how the king is going to find his new queen. All of these beautiful young ladies are going to be taken from their families and gathered together at the king's palace. After a year of beauty treatments, each lady will be brought to the king to see if he will choose her to be his queen.

It may sound like fun to be chosen to live in a palace, but these young ladies's lives will totally change. They do not have a choice in the decision to go to the palace. They will have to leave their families behind and live in a totally different environment. They may or may not be chosen to be the new queen.

HOW will one young lady handle this challenge? WHAT will she do? We'll find out as we keep uncovering the truth in God's story about Esther.

Great research! Now look at the next puzzle. Find the correct path through the maze by beginning at "Start" to find this week's memory verse. After you find the correct path, fill in the blanks with the words in the correct order from the maze.

Then look at Esther 2, find the reference for this verse and write it in. Practice saying this verse out loud three times in a row, three times every day this week!

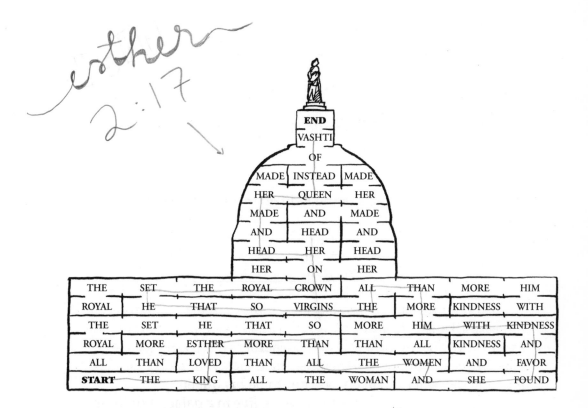

"The king loved Esther more than all the women, and she found favor and kindness with him more than all the virgins, so that he set the royal crown on her head and made her queen instead of vashti."

Esther 2: 17

WHO IS MORDECAI?

"Okay, Molly, tell us a little bit more about the legislative branch of our government that we call the United States Congress," Uncle Matt requested.

"The U.S. Congress is made up of two parts: the House of Representatives and the Senate. The total number of House of Representative members for each state is based on how many people live in that state. Each member represents an area of the state called a congressional district. The number of representatives is based on the number of districts in each state. So states that have large populations have more representatives than smaller states. But every state has at least one representative in the House. A member of the House of Representatives is called a congressman or a congresswoman and is elected to serve in Congress for two years. When the two years are over, new members of Congress are elected or previous members are reelected."

"Good work, Molly. Max, what about the Senate?"

"Well," Max said, "the Senate is different from the House because every state has two senators no matter how big or small the state. Every senator serves a term of six years. When a senator's term is over, the people in the state can elect a new senator or keep the same one to serve another six years. Together, the congressmen and congresswomen and the senators who make up these two parts of the government—the House and the Senate—make our laws and represent all the American people."

"You two are so sharp!" Uncle Matt smiled. "Now let's head back to Esther. Yesterday we saw that the king had a plan to find a new queen. Today as we continue our research, we need to get a close-up look at a new person in our study—a man named Mordecai. So…"

"We know, Uncle Matt!" Max laughed. "We need to ask God for His help and get to work!"

"You've got it!"

Okay, kids, pray and turn to page 162. Read Esther 2. Look at every place where you colored a reference to Mordecai blue and make a list of what you discover about this man.

My List on Mordecai

Esther 2:5 Mordecai is a J e w. He is the son of Jair, who is the son of Shimei, who is the son of Kish, who is a Benjamite.

Esther 2:6 Mordecai's great-grandfather Kish was taken into exile from Jerusalem with the _____ who had been exiled with Jeconiah, king of Judah, who had been exiled by King Nebucanezzar.

Esther 2:7 Mordecai was bringing up Hadassah (Esther), his unclesdaughter Mordecai took Hadassah as his own daughter.

Esther 2:10 Mordecai instructed Esther not to make known her people or her kindred.

Esther 2:11 Every day Mordecai walked back and forth in front of the gate of the palace to know how she was and how she fared.

Esther 2:19 Mordecai sat at the king's gate.

Esther 2:20 Mordecai commanded Esther not to make known her kindred or her people.

Esther 2:21-22 While Mordecai was sitting at the king's gate, a plan to lay hands on king Ahasuris was made known to Mordecai, and Mordecai told Queen Haddasah.

Just look at what you uncovered today about Mordecai. You have discovered that he is a Jew, one of God's chosen people, and his great-grandfather Kish left Judah because he was taken into captivity by King Nebuchadnezzar. Tomorrow we will step back in history to get a few more details about how the Jews ended up in the kingdom of the Medes and Persians.

Don't forget to practice your memory verse!

A LOOK BACK IN HISTORY

Yesterday as we did our research on Esther 2, we got a close look at a Jew named Mordecai, whose great-grandfather was taken into captivity by Nebuchadnezzar, the king of Babylon.

How did Mordecai's family end up in the kingdom of the Medes and the Persians if they were taken into captivity by the Babylonians? If you have studied the book of Daniel in the Discover 4 Yourself Bible study *You're a Brave Man, Daniel,* you may remember how the Medes and the Persians took over the Babylonian kingdom. But in case you haven't studied Daniel yet, let's take a trip back in history to uncover more details on Mordecai's people, the sons of Israel.

First, talk to God. Then use your Bible to look up the following Scripture verses and solve the crossword puzzle on page 47. Look up and read Daniel 1:1-2.

Daniel 1:1 WHAT did Nebuchadnezzar come to Jerusalem to do?

1. (Down) To _besiege_ the city

Daniel 1:2 WHAT did the Lord do?

2. (Down) The Lord _gave_ Jehoiakim king of Judah into Nebuchadnezzar's hand with some of the

3. (Across) _vessels_ of the house of God.

WHY would God allow His chosen people, the sons of Israel, to be taken captive by their enemies? Look up and read 2 Chronicles 36:5-7.

2 Chronicles 36:5 WHAT did Jehoiakim do?

    4. (Across) He did ___evil___ in the sight of the Lord his God.

Look up and read Jeremiah 25:1-11.

Jeremiah 25:3-4 HOW did the people respond to the word of the Lord?

    5. (Down) They did not ___listen___.

Jeremiah 25:8 WHAT did the Lord of hosts tell all the people of Judah?

    6. (Down) "You have not ___obeyed___ My words."

Jeremiah 25:9 WHAT is the Lord going to do?

    7. (Down) I will send to ___Nebuchanezzar___ king of Babylon, My servant, and bring them against this

    ? 8. (Across) ___land___ and against its

    ? 9. (Across) ___inhabitants___

Jeremiah 25:11 HOW long will they be in captivity and serve the king of Babylon?

    10. (Down) ___SEVENTY___ years

    Now you know how the Jewish people ended up in Babylon. They did not listen to or obey God, so He allowed them to be taken into captivity for 70 years. So how did they end up in the kingdom of the Medes and Persians?

After King Nebuchadnezzar's reign ends, Belshazzar becomes king. In Daniel 5 we learn that Belshazzar holds a feast and praises other gods instead of the one true God. Suddenly the fingers of a man's hand appear and write a message on a wall.

Look up and read Daniel 5:24-31.

> Daniel 5:28 WHAT has God done to the Babylonian kingdom?
>
> 11. (Across) It has been <u>divided</u> and given over to the
>
> 12. (Down) <u>Medes</u> and
>
> 13. (Across) <u>Persians</u>.

> Daniel 5:31 WHO received the kingdom after Belshazzar was slain?
>
> 14. (Across) <u>Darius</u> the Mede

Now turn to Daniel 6 and read verse 28.

> WHAT reign did Daniel enjoy success in?
>
> 15. (Down) The reign of Darius the Mede and the reign of <u>Cyrus</u> the Persian

Now let's look at the time chart to see some events that happened from the Jewish captivity through the time of the Medo-Persian kingdom. Look under "Medo-Persian Kings" on the next page. WHAT do we see about the exiles?

There are three returns from exile.

Some of the Jews who were living in the Medo-Persian kingdom returned to Jerusalem after the 70 years of captivity. Find the circled 1 on the time chart and answer the questions.

THE TIMES OF EZRA, NEHEMIAH, AND ESTHER

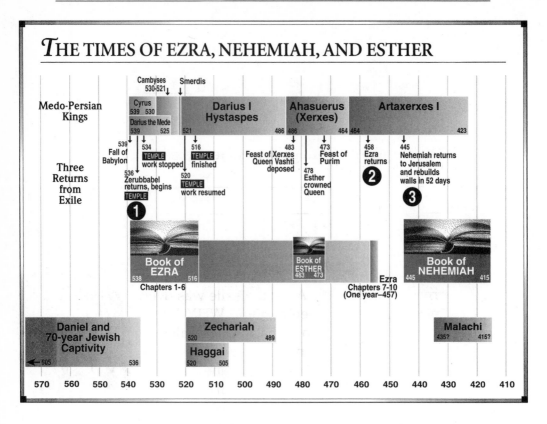

WHO was one of the Jews who returned home to Jerusalem? _Zerrubbabel_

WHAT did he begin rebuilding? The t_emple_

WHEN was this building finished? __516__ B.C.

WHEN does the book of Esther take place?

__483__ to __473__ B.C.

WHO is the king? King __Ahasurus__

WHAT is his other name? __Xerxes__

Look up and read Ezra 1:5.

WHO returned to Jerusalem?

Everyone whose ___heart___ God ___moved___

to go up

WHY didn't Mordecai go back to Jerusalem?

___his heart wasn't___
___moved.___

Now you know why Mordecai was living in the kingdom of the Medes and Persians while other Jews had returned to Jerusalem. After the exile was over, God did not stir his heart to return home. WHY didn't God stir Mordecai's heart to go back to Jerusalem? We don't know, but we do know God always has a reason and a plan for the things He does and doesn't do. God is sovereign. That means He is in control of everything! God had a reason for Mordecai to be at the citadel in Susa at that time in history.

Let's look at one more passage of Scripture. Yesterday when we made our list on Mordecai, we saw that he took his uncle's daughter, Hadassah (Esther), as his own daughter after her family died. When Esther was going to be taken to the king's palace, her cousin told her *not* to make her people known to the king. WHY wouldn't Mordecai want the king to know that Esther is a Jew?

Look up and read Ezra 4:6.

Ezra 4:6 WHAT happened during the reign of Ahasuerus? WHAT was written about the inhabitants of Judah and Jerusalem?

An ___accusation___

Could it be since there were accusations being made about the Jews that Mordecai was worried about the king knowing Esther was Jewish? We don't know, but we do know that Mordecai asked Esther not to tell anyone who her people were.

Way to go! You have done an awesome job looking at the history of God's chosen people, the Jews, and seeing how God placed Mordecai at this time and place in history. Tomorrow we will get a close-up of Esther to see what we can learn about this young Jewish lady.

Don't forget to practice your memory verse!

AN ORPHANED GIRL

"Okay," Uncle Matt said as Max, Sam, and Molly toured the Capitol building, "did you know that both parts of Congress have to agree in order to make a new law? That's why members of both houses have to talk to each other. Every year, Congress looks at thousands of bills. A bill is like a first draft of a law. When a bill starts in the Senate, one or two senators write the bill, and then it goes to a committee of senators where the bill is studied. The committee can send the bill back with no changes, it can send the bill back with changes, or it can do nothing with the bill, which is called 'tabling it.'

"But if a bill isn't tabled, it is voted on by the entire Senate. If half of the senators votes 'yes,' the bill goes on to the House of Representatives. In the House of Representatives, a House committee studies the bill.

"If they make changes, it goes back to the Senate for approval, and then it goes back to the House. Then the House votes on the bill. If more than half of the members vote 'yes,' the bill goes to the president.

"If the president signs the bill, it becomes a law. But if he rejects it, the bill goes back to Congress. This time two-thirds of the House and two-thirds of the Senate must vote in favor of it. If they do, the bill becomes a law. If they don't, the bill dies."

"Whew!" Max said. "It doesn't sound like an easy job to get all those people to agree to make a bill a law."

"It's not. That's why you will see a lot of arguing back and forth when we are sitting in the gallery watching Congress in session. But that's also the reason the Founding Fathers made our government this way—so we would have to work together to do what is best for the people in our country."

Now that we have looked at how the laws are made in our country, let's head back to the kingdom of the Medes and Persians. Today we get to take a close look at Esther.

Ask God for His help, and then turn to page 162. Read Esther 2. Let's make a list on Esther. Look at every place where you colored references to Esther pink in Esther 2, and fill in the list on what you discover about this young lady.

My List on Esther

Esther 2:7 Esther's father and mother d i e d so Mordecai took her as his own daughter. Esther (Hadassah) was beautiful of form and face.

Esther 2:8 Esther was taken to the k i n g's palace into the custody of Hegai.

Esther 2:9 Esther p l e a s e d Hegai and found favor with him. She was given cosemetics and food, and seven choice _maids_ from the king's palace. Esther was transferred to the _best_ place in the _harem_.

Esther 2:10 "Esther did not make _known_ her _people_ or her _kindred_."

Esther 2:15 Esther was the daughter of _Abihail_, the uncle of _Mordecai_, who took her as his _daughter_. When Esther went in to see the king, she did not _request_ anything except what Hegai _advised_. Esther found _favor_ in the _eyes_ of _all_ who _saw_ her.

Esther 2:16 Esther was taken to _King Ahasurus_ to his _royal palace_ in the _10th_ month, in the _7th_ year of the king's reign.

Esther 2:17 The king _loved_ Esther more than _all_ the _women_. Esther found _favor_ and _kindness_ with the king more than all the _virgins_. The king put the _royal crown_ on Esther's head and made her _Queen_.

Esther 2:18 Esther is given a __banquet__ by the king.

Esther 2:20 Esther did not make __known__ her __people__ or her __kindred__, for Esther __did__ what Mordecai told her as she had done when under Mordecai's __care__.

Esther 2:22 Esther informs the k__ing__ in Mordecai's __name__ about the p__lot__.

There is a new queen! Look back at Esther 2:16.

Esther 2:16 WHEN was Esther taken to see the king?

The ___10th___ month in the ___7th___

year of the reign of King Ahasuerus

That means it has been four years from when Vashti was queen until Esther is taken to see the king. WHAT else did we discover in our list? Look at Esther 2:18.

Esther 2:18 WHAT did the king give Esther?

___a banquet___

___

Make a list on this event in Esther 2.

Banquet #4
Esther's Banquet

Esther 2:18 The ___king___ gave Esther a ___great___ banquet for all his ___servants___ and his ___princes___. The king made a ___holiday___ for the ___provinces___ and gave ___gifts___ according to his ___bounty___.

Go back over your list on Esther and think about all the things you have discovered about this young orphan girl who becomes a queen.

Tomorrow we will look at Queen Vashti and Queen Esther to find out how they are alike and how they are different.

Don't forget to practice your memory verse!

Then we'll head to the gallery to watch Congress work for our country.

DAY FIVE

A LOOK AT THE QUEENS

You have done an awesome job this week as you took a look at the United States Congress at work on Capitol Hill and the people and events in the book of Esther. Yesterday we took a close look at Esther, the new queen. Today we need to think about what we learned about both Queen Vashti and Queen Esther. HOW are they alike? HOW are they different?

Let's find out. First, ask God for His help. Now turn to page 161. HOW are Queen Esther and Queen Vashti alike?

> Esther 1:11 WHAT did the king want to display to the people and princes?
>
> Queen Vashti's _beauty_

> Esther 2:7 HOW is Esther described?
>
> _beautiful_ of form and _face_

WHAT did both of the queens have?

Esther 1:9 Queen Vashti gave a _banquet_.

Esther 2:18 The king gave Esther a _banquet_.

Now let's find out HOW they are different. Let's contrast the two queens. A *contrast* shows how two things are different or opposite, such as light and darkness or truth and lies.

Vashti	**Esther**
Esther 1:12,16	*Esther 2:15*
_____	_____
_____	_____
Esther 1:17	*Esther 2:20*
_____	_____
_____	_____
Esther 1:19	*Esther 2:17*
_____	_____
	_____

Amazing! Both queens are beautiful on the outside, but both queens are not beautiful on the inside. Vashti wrongs the king and the people with her behavior and sparks the king's anger. Esther finds favor with everyone. Her character is so special that everyone notices it. Hegai takes special care of her, the king loves her, and Mordecai watches after her even after she is taken into the palace.

We never see Esther show anger or bitterness over the loss of her parents or for being taken from her home and to a new place to live.

And while Vashti disobeys the king, we see Esther obey Mordecai and do all he tells her to do. She listens to the advice of Hegai, who is in charge of the women. Esther is humble. She is respectful and listens to those in authority over her. She has a teachable heart. What an awesome young lady!

How about you? Whose character traits do you see in your life? Are you most like Vashti or Esther? ___Esther___

Do you find favor with people like Esther did? ___yes___

Does your behavior please God, your King?

___✗___ Yes ___ No ___ Sometimes

Name one way you please God.

I listen to Him and obey.

Are you teachable? Do you listen to those whom God has put in your life to teach and help you? Name one way you are teachable. How have you listened to the advice of your parents or teachers?

yes, my mom. as soon as I am wrong, I fix it. I listen when I accidentaly do the opposite.

Think about the things you have learned this week. WHY did God put this beautiful young Jewish lady in the palace with this Persian king at this time in history when there are accusations about the Jews? You'll find out as you continue to do your research. Just remember that God is always present and working behind the scenes.

Don't forget to find a grown-up and say your memory verse out loud!

3

AN EVIL DECREE

ESTHER 3—4

Wasn't it exciting watching Congress at work on Capitol Hill last week and discovering how King Ahasuerus would find his new queen? You also met a Jew named Mordecai and found out why there were Jews living in the kingdom of the Medes and Persians at that time in history. And you met Mordecai's young cousin, Esther, whom he is raising as his daughter.

Esther is one of the young ladies who is taken to the king's palace. Esther is so special that she finds favor with everyone and is chosen by the king to be his new queen. After she becomes the queen, Mordecai uncovers a plot to kill the king. He tells Esther, and Esther tells the king. The men who planned the plot are hanged.

WHAT will happen next in the kingdom? Let's head back to Esther and find out.

DAY ONE

THE KING PROMOTES HAMAN

Uncle Matt smiled at Max and Molly as he kept his hands behind his back.

58

"What's behind your back, Uncle Matt?" Max asked as Sam ran around and jumped up to grab what was in Uncle Matt's hands.

"Calm down, Sam. You'll find out in just a minute. Okay you two, last week we went to the Capitol building to learn about the legislative branch of our government. This week we are going to learn about another branch of our government: the executive branch."

"All right!" Molly squealed. "The executive branch is the president of the United States!"

"So, Uncle Matt..." Max grinned. "Does what you have behind your back have something to do with the president?"

"It sure does! Are you ready for a big surprise?" Uncle Matt asked as he handed Max an envelope with the presidential seal on the outside.

Max, Molly, and Sam

"I can't believe it!" Max exclaimed as he opened the invitation and read it out loud. "Molly, we've been invited to the White House! And not just the White House, but we get to meet the president inside the Oval Office. How terrific is that! Uncle Matt, you are the best!"

Max and Molly jumped up and high-fived Uncle Matt while Sam nipped at Uncle Matt's legs to get in on the action.

"Do we get to go today?" Molly asked.

"Not today. Be patient," Uncle Matt said. "I have a few more tricks up my sleeve. You kids are getting to do something very few people get to do because the president and I are friends. Just hang in there. Besides, we haven't done our research on Esther today. Let's talk to God and find out what is happening in the city of Susa now that Esther has become the queen."

Turn to page 164. Read Esther 3:1-6 and mark the following key words on your Observation Worksheet. Add any new words to your key-word bookmark.

King Ahasuerus (king) (color it orange)

Mordecai (color it blue)

Jew (draw a blue Star of David like this: ✡   )

Haman (the son of Hammedatha the Agagite) (box it in black)

rage (color it red)

destroy (draw a black squiggly line like this: ⌇⌇⌇⌇⌇)

Don't forget to mark the pronouns! And mark anything that tells you WHEN by drawing a green clock 🕐 or green circle like this: ◯ .

Let's find out what is happening in the kingdom. Ask the 5 W's and an H.

Esther 3:1 WHEN is this happening?

after these events

Since Esther 3 takes place after the events in Esther 2, let's review what happened in Esther 2.

Esther 2:17 WHO became queen? _Esther_

Esther 2:21-22 WHAT did Mordecai make known to Queen Esther?

A _plot_ to kill King Ahasuerus

Esther 3:1 WHAT does King Ahasuerus do after these events?

promotes Haman

Esther 3:1 WHO is Haman?

son of Ammede-tha the agagite

Esther 3:2 WHAT did all the king's servants who were at the king's gate do?

paid and bowed down to Haman

Ester 3:2 WHO didn't bow down, or honor, Haman?

Mordecai

Esther 3:3-4 WHY did Mordecai refuse to follow—to transgress—the king's command? WHY wouldn't Mordecai bow down to Haman?

Because he was a _Jew_

Esther 3:5 HOW does Haman react when he sees Mordecai won't bow down and pay homage to him?

he was filled with rage

Esther 3:6 WHAT does Haman seek to do?

kill all jews

Great work! Just look at all you discovered! You have seen a new character come on the scene: a man named Haman. He is the son of Hammedatha the Agagite. Haman was put in a place of authority by the king. Haman is filled with rage because Mordecai won't bow down to him so he wants to kill all the Jews.

HOW will Haman get rid of Mordecai and the rest of the Jews? We'll find out tomorrow.

Before you leave today, discover this week's memory verse by looking at the presidential seal. Some of the stars on this drawing of the seal have numbers under them. Look at the blanks on the next page and find the letter in the star on the seal that matches the number under each blank. Fill in the blanks with the correct letter. Then look at Esther 4 to find the correct reference for this verse and fill it in.

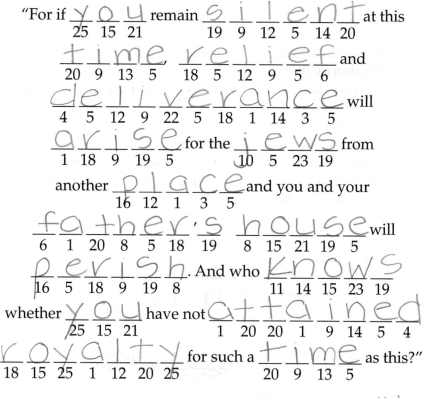

"For if y o u remain s i l e n t at this
25 15 21   19 9 12 5 14 20

t i m e, r e l i e f and
20 9 13 5   18 5 12 9 5 6

d e l i v e r a n c e will
4 5 12 9 22 5 18 1 14 3 5

a r i s e for the j e w s from
1 18 9 19 5   10 5 23 19

another p l a c e and you and your
16 12 1 3 5

f a t h e r ' s h o u s e will
6 1 20 8 5 18 19   8 15 21 19 5

p e r i s h. And who k n o w s
16 5 18 9 19 8   11 14 15 23 19

whether y o u have not a t t a i n e d
25 15 21   1 20 20 1 9 14 5 4

r o y a l t y for such a t i m e as this?"
18 15 25 1 12 20 25   20 9 13 5

Esther 4: 14

Way to go! Write this verse on an index card and practice saying it out loud three times in a row, three times today!

DAY TWO

A DECREE IS MADE

"Now," Uncle Matt said, "before we head to the White House to meet the president, let's talk about the executive branch of the government. Max, you start."

"The president of the United States is the head of the executive branch of our government. His job is to approve bills that Congress creates. If he agrees with the bill, he signs it and it becomes a law. If he doesn't like a bill, he can refuse to sign it. This is called a veto. If the president vetoes a bill, it probably won't become a law unless two-thirds of the members of Congress override the president's decision."

"And," Molly added, "the president also acts as the head of state. That means he meets with the leaders of other countries and makes treaties with them. But the Senate must approve any treaty before it becomes a law. He is also the chief of the government, which means he is the boss of every government worker."

"Don't forget," added Max, "the president is also the commander in chief of the armed forces. That means he is the head of the U.S. military and can authorize the use of troops overseas without declaring war. To officially declare war, he has to get the approval of Congress.

"The president also has a cabinet. The cabinet's job is to advise the president. The cabinet is a group of the president's closest and most trusted advisers, including the vice president. They meet at least once a week to discuss matters that affect the United States."

"Very good, you two!" Uncle Matt exclaimed. "I think you are ready to meet the president."

"But," Max quickly added, "is the president ready to meet Sam?"

Uncle Matt and Molly cracked up laughing while Sam jumped up to give Max a good lick on the face.

"Okay!" Uncle Matt smiled as he took control. "Tomorrow is the *big* day. Today we need to continue our work in Esther 3. Let's grab our colored pencils and ask God for His help as we get to work."

Turn to page 165. Read Esther 3:7-15 and mark the following key words on your Observation Worksheet. Add any new words to your key-word bookmark.

King Ahasuerus (king) (color it orange)

Jew (draw a blue Star of David like this: ✡)

Haman (the son of Hammedatha the Agagite) (box it in black)

edict (decree, decreed) (box it in purple)

destroy (destruction, annihilate) (draw a black squiggly line like this: ~~~~~~)

enemy (circle it in red)

Don't forget to mark the pronouns! And mark anything that tells you WHERE by double-underlining the WHERE in green. Mark anything that tells you WHEN by drawing a green clock or green circle like this: ◯ .

Let's find out Haman's plan to get rid of Mordecai and the Jews. Ask the 5 W's and an H.

Esther 3:7 WHEN is this happening? WHAT year is it in the reign of King Ahasuerus?

In the ___twelfth___ year

(Esther has been queen for five years.)

Esther 3:7 WHAT is cast before Haman?

___pur, a lot___

Do you know what it means to cast lots? Take a look at the information in the box to find out.

Casting Lots

In the Old Testament, people cast lots to decide things. God sometimes used these lots to reveal truth to His people. Lots were small bits of wood or stone. Sometimes the names of people were written on the stones. The stones were placed in a container and shaken together. The first lot to fall out showed who was chosen.

Esther 3:7 WHEN was the lot cast?

In the _first_ month, which is _Nisan_,
in the _twelfth_ year of King Ahasuerus,
from _day_ to _day_ and _month_
to _month_, until the _twelfth_ month
Adar

Haman is casting lots to find out when is the best time to get rid of the Jews.

Esther 3:8 WHAT does Haman tell King Ahasuerus about the Jews?

"there are people in all your kindom that believe the opposite of your law."

Esther 3:9 WHAT does Haman want the king to decree?

"they be destroyed"

Esther 3:9 WHAT will Haman pay the king if he makes this decree?

10,000 talents

Esther 3:10 WHAT does the king do?

gave Haman his ring.

WHAT is the importance of a king's signet ring? Take a look at a document Molly discovered:

The King's Ring

The king's signet ring was used to authenticate a document. It was like the king's signature.

The king's ring carried the highest authority and gave the person who had the ring the power to act for the king.

In Genesis 41, Pharaoh gave his signet ring to Joseph to show that he had placed Joseph second in command over the land of Egypt.

King Ahasuerus has just given Haman his signet ring, which means Haman has the power and authority of the king.

Esther 3:10 WHAT do we learn about Haman?

He is the ___son___ of ___Hammadatha___ the ___agagite___, the ___enemy___ of the ___Jews___.

Esther 3:11 WHAT does the king say to Haman?

"The ___silver___ is yours, and the ___people___ also, to ___do___ with them as you ___wish___."

Esther 3:12 WHEN are the king's scribes summoned?

On the ___thirteenth___ day of the ___first___ month

Esther 3:12 HOW was this decree written?

It was written as ___Haman___ commanded, in the name of ___King Ahasurus___ and sealed with the ___king's signet ring___.

Esther 3:13 WHERE were the letters sent?

___couriers in all his___
___provinces___

Esther 3:13 WHAT did the letters say?

To ___destroy___, to ___kill___, and to ___annihelate___ all the ___Jews___, both ___young___ and ___old___, ___women___ and ___children___, in ___one___ day, and to seize their ___possesions___ as plunder

Esther 3:13 WHEN will this happen? When will the Jews be destroyed?

The _thirteenth_ day of the _twelfth_ month

Look back at when the letters were written in Esther 3:12. HOW long do the Jews have from when the letters were written until they as a people are destroyed?

eleven months

Esther 3:14 WHAT do we learn about the edict?

a copy of each in all provinces, so they are ready

Do you remember what we learned about the first edict in Esther 1:19? Take a look back on page 31.

Esther 1:19 WHAT do you see about a royal edict that is issued by the king?

It is written in the _laws_ of _Persia_ and _Media_ so that it cannot be _repealed_

This means that, according to the law of the Medes and the Persians, once an edict is made it cannot be changed.

Esther 3:15 WHAT do the king and Haman do when this decree was issued?

have a drink

Esther 3:15 WHAT is happening in the city of Susa?

they are in confusion

Are you shocked to see that Haman gets the king to sign a decree that will destroy all the Jews? Remember, at this time the king doesn't know that the queen he loves is a Jew. The king has just signed a law that *cannot be changed*. It says all the Jews can be killed—including the woman he loves.

Have you ever had someone hurt your feelings or do something mean to you? Write out what happened.

I am bullied.

Did you think, "Where is God?" and "Why is He letting this happen?" yes

Remember, when it seems like there is no hope, God is in heaven. He sees and knows everything. And He loves you. He works in all circumstances. Sometimes we have to be patient and trust Him. God has a plan!

So WHY would Haman do such an evil thing to the Jews? WHAT will happen to Esther and Mordecai? Tomorrow we will do a little more research to find out.

Don't forget to practice your memory verse!

DAY THREE

DECISION POINTS

"We're here," Uncle Matt announced as they cleared security, entered the White House, and headed to the Oval Office in the west wing.

The president's aide met them outside the door. "It's good to see you again, Matt. The president will be with you in just a moment."

A few minutes later the president's aide opened the door to the Oval Office and announced, "Mr. President, your guests are here."

"Come in! Matt, it's good to have you back in the White House. I hear you are doing quite a job out in the field on your missions."

"Thank you, sir. I would like you to meet my niece Molly, my nephew Max, and the one and only Sam."

Sam tried to jump out of Max's arms to greet the president with a good face-licking, but Max held on tight.

After the president shook Max and Molly's hands, he patted Sam on the head. "It's nice to meet all three of you. Matt has told me all about you and your Bible adventures. I am so proud to know you are studying the Bible and learning how to be leaders. I would like to see the work you are doing in Esther. Why don't you have a seat and show me what you are learning?"

"It would be an honor, Mr. President," Max said as they all sat down. "Would you like to pray for us before we get started?"

"Yes, I would," the president replied as they bowed their heads.

After they prayed, Max and Molly opened their books.

Yesterday as we worked in Esther 3, we saw Haman convince the king to sign a decree that would destroy all the Jews. Today we need to do a little more research to see WHY this happened. Turn to page 164. Read Esther 3:1-10. Let's find out why Haman wanted to destroy Mordecai and all the Jews by asking the 5 W's and an H.

Esther 3:1 WHO was Haman?

He was the __son__ of __Hamm__ the

_____.

Esther 3:1 WHAT did King Ahasuerus do for Haman?

He _____ Haman and advanced him and

established his _____ over all the princes

who were with him.

Esther 3:2 WHO wouldn't bow down to Haman?

_____

Esther 3:4 WHAT was Mordecai's reason?

He was a _____.

Esther 3:5 HOW does Haman react when Mordecai won't bow down?

He is filled with _____.

Esther 3:6 WHOM does Haman want to destroy?

M __ __ __ __ __ __ __ and all the _____, the

_____ of _____

Esther 3:10 HOW is Haman described?

The son of Hammedatha the _____, the

_____ of the Jews

Are you surprised to see Mordecai, a man who is loyal to the king, disobey the king's command to bow down to Haman? Mordecai says it is because he is a Jew. Is that a good reason? Let's find out by looking back at the history of the sons of Israel. God has shown us two times in the first ten verses of Esther 3 that Haman is an Agagite, which means God wants us to understand who Haman is.

WHO are the Agagites? They are the children or descendants of Agag. Since we just saw that the Agagites are enemies of the Jews, let's find out more about Agag and his descendants by doing some *cross-referencing*. Cross-referencing is where we compare Scripture with Scripture. Remember, Scripture is the best interpreter of Scripture!

Look up and read 1 Samuel 15:1-18.

1 Samuel 15:1 WHO was anointed king over God's people?

_____

1 Samuel 15:1 WHAT does Samuel tell Saul to do?

To _____ to the words of the _____

1 Samuel 15:2 WHO will God punish for what they did to Israel?

_____

1 Samuel 15:3 WHAT does God tell Saul to do?

"Go and strike _____ and utterly

_____ all that he has, and do not

_____ him; but put to _____ both

man and woman, child and infant, ox and sheep,

camel and donkey."

1 Samuel 15:8 WHOM did Saul capture?

_____ the _____ of the _____

1 Samuel 15:9 WHAT did Saul do?

He spared _____ and the _____ of the

sheep, the oxen, the fatlings, the lambs, and all

that was _____ and was not _____ to

_____ them utterly.

1 Samuel 15:10-11 WHAT did God say?

"I regret that I have made _____ king, for he

has _____ back from _____ Me and

has not carried out My _____."

1 Samuel 15:18 WHAT mission did God give Saul?

To utterly _____ the sinners, the

_____, and fight against them until

they are_____

Did Saul obey? Did he destroy all the Amalekites?

_____

You have discovered that Agag was the king of the Amalekites. Remember, God wanted Saul to destroy Agag and all the Amalekites. But instead of obeying God's command, Saul disobeyed God. He only did part of what God told him to do. So God rejected Saul as king over Israel.

Think about this for a minute. From what you just learned about Saul, how does God feel about *partial* obedience (doing only part of what He says to do)? Did God say, "Okay, Saul, you did most of what I told you to do, so that's okay"? No way! You have just seen that obeying only partway is disobedience. Obedience is doing *all* of what God says.

How about you? Have there been times when your mom and dad told you to do something and you only did part of what they asked you to do? Write out one time that this happened. Include what they asked you to do and what you did.

_____

_____

_____

_____

Remember what happened to Saul the next time your parents ask you to do something or when you remember what God has told you to do through His Word. *Decide to obey all the way.* Ask God for His help. He will help you!

All right! Now, let's go back to Agag. Since Agag was the king of the Amalekites, it's possible that the term *Agagite* could be a synonym for Amalekite. Remember, synonyms are different words that mean the same thing. Since we have seen that Agag is the king of the Amalekites, let's go back a little further and see what we can learn about the Amalekites.

Look up and read Exodus 17:8-16.

Exodus 17:8 WHO fought against Israel at Rephidim?

_____

Exodus 17:14 WHAT did the Lord say to Moses?

"Write this in a book as a memorial and _____

it to Joshua, that I will utterly _____

_____ the memory of _____

from under heaven."

Exodus 17:16 WHAT did the Lord swear?

He "will have _____ against _____

from generation to generation."

Go back to page 71 and find all the words from the single word blanks on pages 71-75 and circle them in the word search on the next page. If a word is used more than once, you only have to find and circle it one time.

O	Y	U	A	M	A	E	A	Y	H	C	M	G	S	T
H	U	O	E	H	L	M	T	G	O	J	O	N	E	U
K	T	Z	R	P	T	i	A	M	A	U	R	i	T	R
i	B	A	O	T	R	A	M	L	D	G	D	L	i	N
N	P	E	E	O	S	A	D	R	E	T	E	L	K	E
G	P	H	H	D	N	E	P	E	O	K	C	i	E	D
O	U	T	Z	D	M	C	D	R	M	G	A	W	L	Z
F	U	B	S	E	R	A	P	S	O	M	i	P	A	S
A	F	O	L	L	O	W	i	N	G	M	A	N	M	W
J	E	W	E	T	i	G	A	G	A	R	O	H	A	E
L	i	S	T	E	N	N	B	E	B	S	G	T	N	J
D	E	T	A	N	i	M	R	E	T	X	E	E	L	L
Y	D	O	O	G	F	J	S	W	A	R	M	G	U	D
T	L	O	R	D	R	T	X	K	D	Y	G	A	R	B
M	E	T	i	C	E	R	B	L	O	T	S	R	B	T

Great work! Now that you have discovered who Agag and the Amalekites are, if Haman was an Amalekite, would Mordecai have a good reason to refuse the king's command and not bow down to Haman? _____

Think about what God said about the Amalekites in Exodus 17. Write down WHY you think Mordecai did or didn't have a good reason not to bow down to Haman.

_____

_____

_____

WHY do you think Haman would want all the Jews destroyed and not just Mordecai?

_____

_____

Mordecai loves and honors God. He has chosen to not bow down to Haman because Haman is an enemy of God. Mordecai chooses to please God and honor Him rather than honor His enemy.

How about you? Have you made up your mind to honor and live for God? There will be kids who will want you to talk like them, dress like them, and listen to the music they do. They will pressure you to be like them instead of being the person Jesus wants you to be.

What will you do? Will you bow to this world you live in? Will you use words like everyone else uses, even if those words don't please God? _____

Will you wear clothes that show too much of your body or have sayings on them that don't please God? Or are you willing to live your life to please Jesus—even if you are made fun of or have to die for what you believe? _____

Is there a reason, a standard, for what you will and won't do? Mordecai's reason was that he was a Jew. He lived for God. He would not bow down to God's enemy. What is your reason? Write out what you won't do because you want to please God.

_____

_____

_____

What do you think will happen now that the decree has been sent out? HOW will Mordecai react, and WHAT will Esther do? We'll find out soon.

Don't forget to practice your memory verse. They are Mordecai's words to Esther.

DISTRESS IN THE KINGDOM

"I can't believe that we not only got to meet the president, but we also got to work with him in the Oval Office! That was just too cool," Max said.

"And it isn't over yet!" Uncle Matt smiled as he continued. "The president has invited you to sit in when he meets with his cabinet."

"Wow!" exclaimed Molly. "I can't wait to meet all his top advisers."

"Well," Uncle Matt cautioned, "they have a lot of important matters on the agenda, but the president was impressed with your desire to understand how the government works, so he is going to let us visit for just a few minutes. But before we go…"

"We know," Molly said, jumping into the conversation. "We need to find out how Mordecai and Esther react to the new decree."

"You've got it!"

Don't forget to talk to God. Then turn to page 166. Read Esther 4 and mark the following key words on your Observation Worksheet. Add any new words to your key-word bookmark.

king (color it orange)

Mordecai (color it blue)

Jew (draw a blue Star of David like this: ✡)

Esther (queen) (color it pink)

favor (color it yellow)

Haman (the son of Hammedatha the Agagite) (box it in black)

mourn (circle it in red and color it black)

sackcloth (draw a black arch like this: ⌒)

ashes (color it black)

wail (wailing, weeping) (circle it in blue)

fast (fasting) (color it brown)

perish (box it in red)

edict (decree, decreed) (box it in purple)

destroy (destruction, annihilate) (draw a black squiggly line like this: ～～～～)

Don't forget to mark the pronouns! And mark anything that tells you WHERE by double-underlining the WHERE in green. Mark anything that tells you WHEN by drawing a green clock or green circle like this: ⃝ .

Now let's ask those 5 W's and an H.

Esther 4:1 WHAT did Mordecai do when he learned about all that had been done?

_____

_____

_____

Esther 4:2 HOW far did Mordecai go?

_____

_____

Esther 4:2 WHY didn't he enter the king's gate?

_____

Esther 4:3 WHAT happened in every province where
the command and decree of the king went?

There was great _____ among the

_____ with _____, _____, and

_____; and many lay on _____

and _____.

Esther 4:4 WHAT did Esther do when her maids and
her eunuchs told her what was happening?

_____

Esther 4:4 WHY did she send clothes to Mordecai?

_____

Esther 4:4 WHAT did Mordecai do?

_____

Esther 4:5 WHY did Esther send Hathach to Mordecai?

_____

Esther 4:7 WHAT did Mordecai tell Hathach?

_____

_____

Esther 4:8 WHAT did Mordecai give Hathach?

_____

Esther 4:8 WHY did Mordecai want Esther to have a copy of the edict?

To _____ her so she would go to the _____ to implore his _____ and to _____ with him for her _____

Esther 4:11 WHY was Esther afraid to go to the king?

_____

_____

Esther 4:13-14 WHAT did Mordecai tell Esther?

"Do not imagine that _____ in the _____ palace can _____ any more than all the _____. For if you remain _____ at this time, _____ and _____ will _____ for the _____ from another place and _____ and your _____ _____ will _____. And who knows whether you have not _____ _____ for such a _____ as this?"

Esther 4:16 HOW did Esther respond to Mordecai's message?

"Go, _____ all the _____ who are found in Susa, and _____ for me; do not _____ or _____ for _____ days, night or day. I and my _____ also will _____ in the same way. And thus I will go

in to the _____, which is not according to
the _____; and if I _____, I _____."

Esther 4:17 WHAT did Mordecai do?

_____

_____

Did you notice that Esther can't go to see the king unless she is summoned by him? And for the last 30 days the king has not asked to see her. WHAT is the law if she goes to the king without being summoned? Unless the king holds out his golden scepter to her, she will be killed.

Mordecai loves Esther like his own daughter. He knows what may happen to Esther if she goes to the king, but Mordecai loves his people so much he is willing to risk losing Esther to save his nation.

Can you imagine being asked to do something that could lead to your death? Think about all the soldiers who fight for our country. Every day they lay their lives on the line for us. Would you be willing to serve your country like soldiers do?

_____

Do you love Jesus so much that you would be willing to risk your life by sharing the gospel in a place that is dangerous for Christians? _____

Think about this. Is there something or someone you love so much that you would be willing to lay down your life?

_____

WHY does Esther ask Mordecai to have the Jews fast for her before she goes in to see the king? Do you know? We'll find out tomorrow when we take a closer look at fasting and Mordecai's message to Esther.

Don't forget to practice your memory verse!

SACRIFICE FOR A NATION

"I just loved sitting in with the cabinet, Uncle Matt," Molly said as they ate lunch on the National Mall. "Thank you so much for all that you have done to make this such a special adventure for us."

"Hey, you're forgetting how much I love these adventures, too. I'm just sorry that I am usually out on assignment and don't get to do as many with you as Uncle Jake. I am proud of you guys for wanting to serve God so much that you want to learn about serving our country. Now that you have seen our nation's leaders at work, we need to head back to the book of Esther and look at two very important leaders."

Yesterday we saw Mordecai and Esther learn about the edict that has been made to destroy all the Jews. Mordecai tells Esther to go to the king and plead for the lives of her people. But if Esther goes to the king without being asked by him, and if the king doesn't extend his golden scepter toward her, she will be put to death.

Let's look at WHAT Mordecai does when he learns about the edict and HOW the other Jews react when they hear the decree. Talk to God. Then turn to page 166 and read Esther 4. Review by asking the 5 W's and an H.

Esther 4:1 WHAT did Mordecai do when he learned what had been done?

He _____ his _____ and put on _____ and ashes.

Esther 4:3 WHAT did the other Jews do when they heard the decree?

_____

_____

Esther 4:16 WHAT does Esther ask Mordecai to have all the Jews in Susa do?

_____

_____

Let's find out what God's Word has to say about sackcloth, ashes, and fasting. Look up and read Genesis 37:34. This is the first mention of sackcloth in the Bible.

Genesis 37:34 WHY did Jacob tear his clothes and put on sackcloth?

To _____ for his son

Look up and read Genesis 18:27.

WHAT does Abraham say that he is?

_____

Look up and read Jonah 3:4-10.

Jonah 3:5 WHAT did the people of Nineveh do?

They _____ in _____; and they called a _____ and put on _____.

Jonah 3:7-8 WHAT was the king's decree?

"Do not let _____, beast, herd, or flock _____ a thing. Do not let them _____ or _____water...Both _____ and beast must be _____ with _____; and let _____ _____ on _____ earnestly that each may _____ from his _____ way and from the _____ which is in his hands."

Jonah 3:9 WHAT did they hope God would do?

_____

Jonah 3:10 WHAT did God do when He saw their deeds?

_____

Think about what we learned about sackcloth, ashes, and fasting. Jacob mourned his son's death. Abraham humbled himself before God, telling God he was just dust and ashes. The king and people of Nineveh humbled themselves to show God they were sorry for their sins. They hoped God would forgive them and not destroy Nineveh.

Take a look at the following document Max found that tells about sackcloth, fasting, and ashes.

Scratchy Clothes

Sackcloth was a warm, dark material that was woven from goat or camel hair. Garments made of sackcloth felt rough and itchy against a person's skin.

Sackcloth was worn to show sorrow for sins. The harsh texture of the garment reminded the people of how uncomfortable sin should be.

When people wore sackcloth and put ashes on their skin, they usually fasted as well. *Fasting* means they chose not to eat food or drink liquids.

Sackcloth, ashes, and fasting were outward expressions of hearts full of sorrow.

From what you have seen in the Bible, do you understand why Mordecai and the other Jews put on sackcloth and ashes and fasted? Think about WHY Esther wanted all the Jews in Susa, her maidens, and herself to fast before she went to see the king. The Jews' situation looks hopeless. They are going to be destroyed in 11 months. They are facing a situation they have no control over.

WHAT can they do? Look at what the king and the people of Nineveh did. They turned from their wicked ways. They believed in God. They called a fast and put on sackcloth, hoping God would turn from His anger and they would not perish.

God's people know when there is no hope that there is a God in heaven who is in control of *everything!* So they humble themselves before Him in their crisis and go without eating or drinking to seek God's presence and show Him they need and want His help.

Isn't that *awesome?* When they are afraid, when there is no hope, they know they can run to God because He loves them and has the power to change things. No man-made law or evil person can stop God from rescuing His people!

How about you? What do you do when something bad happens and you are afraid?

_____

_____

_____

When something bad happens to you, God knows. He is with you, and He will help you! Write out what you will do the next time something bad or scary happens to you.

_____

_____

Let's look at one more thing in Esther 4. Turn to page 167 and read Esther 4:13-14. Think about what Mordecai is saying to Esther. He is saying, "Don't think that just because you are the queen, you will escape. And if you don't speak out, then God will rescue His people another way." HOW can Mordecai be so confident that God will rescue His people with or without Esther's help? Look up and read Genesis 12:1-3.

Genesis 12:2 WHAT is God going to make Abram?

A _____ _____: "And I will

_____ you, and make your _____

great; and so you will be a _____."

Look up and read Genesis 13:15.

WHAT will God give to Abram and his descendants forever?

_____

The great nation that God made of Abraham is the nation of Israel, the Jews. Mordecai is confident when he tells Esther that God will rescue His people because he knows God's promises. Mordecai has faith.

He tells Esther, "I know deliverance is coming one way or another, but I believe God has chosen to use you." Esther has a choice to make. Will she forget about herself and lay down her life for her people? Or will she do nothing and God will rescue them another way? WHAT did she choose to do?

Esther 4:16 WHAT will Esther do after they have fasted for three days?

"I will _____ in to the _____...and if I

_____, I _____."

Isn't that *amazing?* This young queen is willing to lay down her life for her people. Esther has courage.

How about you? Are you willing to lay down your life for God to use? Say your memory verse out loud to a grown-up and think about Mordecai's words to Esther. Has God put you in your family, your school, and with certain friends because He has a purpose for you? If you aren't willing to let God use you, He can choose someone else. God's purpose will always come to pass no matter what you choose to do, but you will miss out on God's plan and His reward for you!

Ask yourself: "Do I want to live for me or do I want to live for God?" If you decide you want to live for God, then ask Him, "God, how can You use me? What do You want me to do?"

God may want you to reach out to a lonely kid who doesn't have any friends. Or He may want you to be a good example to other kids by the words that you use, the clothes you wear, or what you read or watch on TV. He may want you to show courage, to stand up for what is right, even if you are made fun of and left out. Or maybe He wants you to obey your parents without whining, complaining, or arguing.

Trust God to show you why He has put you in this place at this time in your life, just like He did for Esther. It may not be an easy choice, but God loves you. He will help you do what He says is right. Our world tells us "life is all about *me*," while Jesus tells us there is only one way to be His disciple—that "life is all about Jesus"!

> *If anyone wishes to come after Me, he must deny himself, and take up his cross and follow Me. For whoever wishes to save his life will lose it, but whoever loses his life for My sake and the gospel's will save it* (Mark 8:34-35).

To be Jesus' disciples, we have to die to ourselves and live for Him. We have to be willing to surrender *everything* so God can use us.

In Esther, the fast has begun. WHAT will happen now that Esther is willing to lay down her life for her people? We'll find out next week!

4

A COURAGEOUS QUEEN

ESTHER 5—7

Last week was *amazing!* We met the president of the United States, worked in the Oval Office, sat in with the president and his cabinet, and continued to watch God's story unfold after Esther became queen.

As we continued our study in Esther, we saw an Agagite named Haman convince King Ahasuerus to sign a decree that would destroy all the Jews. Queen Esther is faced with a crisis. Should she risk her life by going before the king to plead for her people even though the king has not summoned her?

After Mordecai tells Esther that God has put her in the kingdom for just this time, Esther decides to lay down her life for her people. She calls for a fast by her people before she goes to see the king. WHAT will happen? Will Esther perish or will the king extend his golden scepter? Let's find out.

DAY ONE

INSIDE THE THRONE ROOM

"Are you ready for your next surprise?" Uncle Matt asked Max and Molly.

"We sure are!" Molly exclaimed, while Sam barked his agreement and gave Molly a big lick. "Ugh, more dog kisses! Yuck, Sam!"

Max and Uncle Matt laughed and gave Sam a thumbs-up pat.

"Well, you two—or should I say three and include Sam?—are going back to the White House. The president was so blown away by how much you have studied and how much you want to learn that he has invited you to a 'you can't miss it' event."

"What is it, Uncle Matt?" Max asked.

"You are invited to a state dinner at the White House, and you get to spend the night in one of the White House bedrooms."

"Are you kidding!" Max exclaimed. "Sam too?"

"Yes—Sam too. The president has a little surprise for Sam— someone he wants him to meet that he thinks can keep Sam on his paws."

"All right!" Molly high-fived Max. "This is going to be so awesome!"

"But first…" Uncle Matt smiled. "First, we need to head back to Esther."

"You got it!" replied Max. "I'll pray so we can get to work."

Turn to page 167. Read Esther 5:1-8 and mark the following key words on your Observation Worksheet. Add any new words to your key-word bookmark.

>   king (color it orange)
>
>   Esther (queen) (color it pink)
>
>   favor (color it yellow)
>
>   Haman (box it in black)
>
>   banquet (circle it in brown)

Don't forget to mark the pronouns! And mark anything that tells you WHEN by drawing a green clock ⏰ or green circle like this: ◯ .

Find out WHAT is happening by asking the 5 W's and an H. Look back at Esther 4:16.

Esther 4:16 HOW many days were the Jews and handmaidens to fast for Esther?

_____ days

Esther 5:1 WHEN is this happening?

On the _____ _____

Esther 5:1 WHAT does Esther do?

_____

_____

Esther 5:2 HOW does the king respond to Esther?

She finds _____ in his sight.

Esther 5:2 WHAT does the king do?

_____

Esther 5:2 WHAT does Esther do?

_____

_____

Esther 5:3 WHAT does the king ask Esther?

_____

_____

Esther 5:3 WHAT will the king do for Esther?

"Even to _____ of the _____

it shall be _____ to you."

Even though the king has not sent for Esther for 33 days, you can see how much he cares about her when she comes before his royal throne. The king extends his golden scepter toward her. He wants to know what is troubling Esther and what he can do for her, even if it means giving her up to half of his kingdom.

Esther 5:4 WHAT does Esther ask the king?

for a banquet

Let's make a list on this fifth banquet in the book of Esther.

Banquet #5

Esther 5:4 WHO is preparing the banquet?

Esther

Esther 5:4 WHO is invited to the banquet?

King A and Haman

Esther 5:6 WHAT did they do at the banquet?

eat and drink

Esther 5:6 WHAT does the king ask Esther at the banquet?

what is her petetion

Esther 5:7-8 WHAT is Esther's petition and request?

another banquet

Think about what you have learned about Esther today. HOW does she handle the situation when she comes before the king? Does she rush in to the king all worried and upset, blurting out her problem? Or does she act calm, confident, and patient? Does she show honor and respect to the king? Write out HOW Esther behaves.

calm, confident, and patient

WHY do you think Esther is calm and courageous when she comes into the king's presence? WHAT has Esther been doing for the last three days?

praying and fasting

Think about what you learned about sackcloth, ashes, and fasting last week. When Esther and all of her people fasted, were they just going without food and drink? Or were they also humbling themselves before God, seeking His help?

humbling before God, seeking His help.

Even though the book of Esther does not say the people sought God or prayed, we know from all we learned about fasting, sackcloth, and ashes in other passages in the Bible that Esther and the Jews are humbling themselves and seeking God's intervention.

They know the one true God. One of God's names is *El Elyon*, which means "God Most High." That means God is sovereign. He is the Ruler over the entire universe! There is absolutely nothing that God does not have complete and total control over.

Isn't that incredible? There is nothing—no edict, no king (evil or good), no evil men or women, and no crisis—that God doesn't know about and cannot change. He is in control of *all* things!

Look at how God has Esther in the right place at the right time to become the new queen, how He places her in a position to go before the king when Haman plots to kill all the Jews. Look at the timing of when the Jews will be killed. They have 11 months to prepare for what is coming. And just look at how calm and courageous Esther is, and how God gives her favor before the king. Isn't it great to see God's hand at work behind the scenes?

All right! You have done a fantastic job! Discover this week's memory verse. Decide which of the missing vowels (a, e, i, o, u) needs to go on each of the blanks inside Queen Esther's crown. Once you have added the vowels to uncover this week's verse, find the reference in Esther 7 and write it on the blank.

"Th_e_n Q_uee_n _E_sth_e_r r_e_pl_i_ed,

'_i_f _i_ h_a_v_e_ f___nd f_v_r _n

y___r s_ght, _ k_ng, _nd _f _t

pl___s_s th_ k_ng, l_t my l_f_

b_ g_v_n m_ _s my p_t_t___n,

_nd my p___pl_ _s my r_q___st.'"

Esther 7: ____

Write this verse on an index card and practice saying it aloud three times in a row, three times a day, every day this week!

HAMAN DEVISES ANOTHER PLAN

"Okay, Uncle Matt," Molly said. "Please tell us about the state dinner at the White House."

"A state dinner is a fancy dinner party that the president throws for a 'head of state' of another country. Most presidents only hold a few of these dinners, so getting an invitation to one is rare and very special.

"This state dinner is to honor the president of Kenya. The dessert will be something really unique to honor that president's country. At the state dinner for the queen of England, there were tiny chocolates in the shape of Big Ben, a famous clock in London."

"Mmmm!" Max licked his lips. "I can't wait! I wonder what the dessert will be to honor Kenya? But what about 'you know who'? With all the special guests and great food, we don't want to cause a national incident if he gets loose."

Uncle Matt laughed. "Don't worry about Sam. The president has a plan for that special guest. Now let's head back to Esther and find out what happens after Esther's banquet for the king and Haman."

Don't forget to talk to God. Then turn to page 168. Read Esther 5:9-14 and mark the following key words on your Observation Worksheet. Add any new words to your key-word bookmark.

    king (color it orange)

    Esther (queen) (color it pink)

    Haman (box it in black)

    banquet (circle it in brown)

    Mordecai (color it blue)

Jew (draw a blue Star of David like this: ✡)

anger (color it red)

Don't forget to mark the pronouns! And mark anything that tells you WHEN by drawing a green clock 🕐 or green circle like this: ○ .

WHAT happens after Haman leaves Esther's banquet? Ask those 5 W's and H.

Esther 5:9 HOW did Haman go out that day?

_____

Esther 5:9 HOW did Haman react when Mordecai did not stand up or tremble before him?

_____

Esther 5:10 WHAT did Haman do?

_____

Esther 5:11 WHAT does Haman recount to his friends and family?

The _____ of his _____, and the

_____ of his _____, and every _____

where the _____ had _____ him and

_____ him above the _____ and

_____ of the king

WHAT is Haman doing? Do you know what this is called? It's b __ __ __ __ __ __ g! Haman is bragging at how great he is and how the king has given him authority in the kingdom. Haman is a man of great pride.

Esther 5:12 WHAT else did Haman brag about?

_____

_____

Esther 5:13 WHAT do we see about Haman?

He is not _____.

WHY? Because of _____

Esther 5:14 WHAT do his wife and all his friends tell Haman?

_____

_____

WHAT does Haman do?

_____

_____

Wow! Think about what you have learned about Haman. This is the man the king promoted and gave his seal to. Haman gets to make decisions for the king. WHAT kind of man is Haman? WHAT is inside his heart? Circle the qualities you see in him:

Anger   Pride   Hatred
Love   Jealousy   Kindness

Do you see any of Haman's qualities in you?

____ Yes   ____ No   ____ Sometimes

Is Haman happy with all that he has? _____ WHY or why not?

_____

_____

Are you satisfied with what you have? Or are you jealous of what other kids have? Do you want to have the biggest, the latest, the most, and the best?

_____

_____

WHAT kind of friends and family does Haman have?

_____

Do his friends and family influence him?_____

WHAT are your friends like?

_____

_____

Do your friends try to get you to do the right things or wrong things?

_____

Do your friends influence your decisions?_____

Are you careful about the friends you choose?_____

Name one of your friends who loves Jesus, who encourages you, and who helps you do what God says is right.

_____

If you don't have a good friend who is a good influence, pray and ask God to help you find someone your age you can reach out to and become good friends with.

Way to go! Tomorrow we get to see God's hand at work in another situation. Don't forget to practice your memory verse!

A SLEEPLESS NIGHT

"Come in!" said one of the president's top aides as he welcomed Matt, Molly, Max, and Sam into the Blue Room inside the White House. He looked at Sam. "Sam, I have a surprise for you! Hold on just one minute."

Max and Molly looked at Uncle Matt, and he grinned.

"Just wait. Sam is going to love this," he said.

Suddenly Max and Molly heard a loud commotion coming down the hall. A young golden retriever skidded into the room and jumped up, putting her two front paws on Max's chest to introduce herself to Sam. A black-and-white border collie came bounding behind her to get in on the action.

"Kate! Sadie! Sit!" the president's aide commanded. After the dogs sat, he said, "Good dogs!" Turning to Matt, Max, Molly, and Sam he said, "Sorry about that. They are both still young, so we are working on their manners. The president and first lady rescued them from an animal shelter. Max, Molly, and Sam, meet Kate and Sadie. Kate is the golden retriever, and Sadie is the border collie. The president thought Sam might like to spend some time playing with them while you are enjoying the state dinner."

Max put Sam down, and Sam ran over to play with Kate and Sadie.

"They like each other. Maybe Kate and Sadie will teach Sam some manners," Max told the aide.

"Or," the aide added, "maybe Sam can teach Kate and Sadie."

"Uh-oh! I don't know about that. The president might make

us leave the country if Sam trains Kate and Sadie. He is always getting in trouble."

Everyone laughed.

"I'll take care of these three wild pups, and someone will escort you to the state dining room for your special dinner. Are you ready to meet the first lady, the president of Kenya, and the other honored guests?"

"We sure are!"

While Max, Molly, and Uncle Matt go to meet the first lady and the president of Kenya, let's find out what happens the night after Esther's banquet. Pray. Then turn to page 168. Read Esther 6 and mark the following key words on your Observation Worksheet. Add any new words to your key-word bookmark.

king (King Ahasuerus) (color it orange)

Mordecai (color it blue)

Jew (draw a blue Star of David like this: ✡)

Haman (box it in black)

mourning (circle it in red and color it black)

Esther (color it pink)

banquet (circle it in brown)

Don't forget to mark your pronouns! And mark anything that tells you WHEN by drawing a 🕐 or green circle like this: ◯ .

Now ask the 5W's and an H to find out WHAT is happening at the palace.

Esther 6:1 WHEN is this happening?

_____

Esther 6:1 WHAT do we see about the king?

_____

_____

Esther 6:1 WHAT does the king do?

_____

Esther 6:2 WHAT did the king find when he read the book of records?

_____

_____

Do you remember this plot to kill the king? Turn to page 164 and read Esther 2:22-23 again.

Esther 2:22 WHAT did Mordecai do?

_____

_____

Esther 2:23 WHAT happened to the men who plotted to kill the king?

_____

Esther 2:23 WHERE was it written?

_____

Can you believe this? The night before Esther's next banquet, Haman is building gallows to hang Mordecai and the king can't sleep.

WHAT does the king do? He has the book of records, the chronicles, read to him. And WHAT does he hear? The plot that Mordecai reported about two eunuchs who wanted to kill him.

Do you think this is a coincidence? Or is God working behind the scenes, keeping the king awake so he will hear about this incident written in the book of records?

Let's go back to Esther 6 on page 168.

Esther 6:3 WHAT does the king ask?

_____

_____

Esther 6:3 WHAT was done for Mordecai?

_____

_____

Esther 6:4 WHAT does the king ask?

_____

_____

Esther 6:4 WHO just entered the court?

_____

_____

Esther 6:4 WHY is Haman at the court?

_____

_____

Esther 6:6 WHAT does the king ask Haman?

_____

_____

Esther 6:6 WHOM does Haman think the king is talk-ing about honoring?

_____

_____

Esther 6:7-9 HOW does Haman tell the king to honor this man?

"Bring a _____ _____ which the

king has worn, and the _____ on

which the king has ridden, and on whose head
a _____ _____ has been placed;
and let the _____ and the _____ be
handed over to one of the king's most _____
_____ and let them _____ the
man whom the king desires to honor and lead
him on _____ through the city
_____, and proclaim before him, 'Thus it
shall be _____ to the man whom the _____
_____ to _____.'"

Esther 6:10 HOW does the king respond to Haman's suggestion?

_____

Esther 6:11 WHAT does Haman do?

_____

_____

_____

Esther 6:12 WHAT does Mordecai do?

_____

Esther 6:12 WHAT does Haman do?

_____

Esther 6:12 WHY is Haman mourning?

_____

Look back at Esther 4:3. WHY were Mordecai and the Jews mourning?

_____

Can you believe Haman is mourning because of his hurt pride in honoring his enemy, while Mordecai and the Jews are mourning because of the decree to destroy them? Can you see the difference? With Haman it's all about him, but with Mordecai it's about others.

Esther 6:13 WHOM does Haman tell about what happened?

_____

_____

Esther 6:13 WHAT does his wise men and wife say to him?

_____

_____

Esther 6:14 WHAT happens next?

_____

_____

Wow! Can you imagine how Haman felt when the king told him to do all those things to honor Mordecai? Here he was thinking, "It's all about *me*. The king wants to honor *me*." So he picks all the things to show himself off. But guess what? It's not about him—it's for Mordecai, a man of honor who didn't complain when his actions to save the king were never rewarded.

Isn't it awesome to see that God rewards people in His perfect time, for His glory and His purpose? God waits until Haman plans to hang Mordecai to remind the king about what Mordecai did for him. God promotes Mordecai at just the right time.

Now ask yourself, "Am I like Haman? Am I full of pride?" What is your answer?

_____

God hates pride because it puts "man" above Him.

How about you? Do you want everything to be all about you? Do you seek to be honored like Haman or to serve God like Mordecai?

_____

Are you happy for your friends when they do well or win awards? Or do you get angry and jealous because it didn't happen to you?

_____

Think about how you act, and write out what you will do the next time one of your friends or classmates is rewarded.

_____

_____

_____

Jesus came to serve and give His life for others. We need to serve God—not seek to be honored. God will honor you in His time, in His way, and for His purpose.

Tomorrow we go to another banquet!

Don't forget to practice your memory verse.

ANOTHER BANQUET

"That was the best and the coolest dinner I have ever had! It was so special of the president to invite us to his state dinner,"

Molly said as Uncle Matt, Max, and she walked outside in the rose garden after dessert. "And I loved those sugar giraffes the chef made to honor the president of Kenya. They were soooo beautiful!"

"Well, Molly, if you go to Kenya," Max teased, "then you can let a real giraffe lick you. Maybe you will like its kisses better than Sam's!"

Before Molly could respond, there was a streak, another streak, and then another streak as three bad dogs named Kate, Sadie, and Sam ran through the garden chasing each other.

"Uh-oh, we better get Kate, Sadie, and Sam before they knock over some of the president's guests."

Whew! Now that Sam, Kate, and Sadie have been caught and given special doggie treats from the president's chef, we can head back to Esther to find out what happens at Esther's next banquet. Are you wondering if they'll have any sugar giraffes or wild pups? Let's find out.

Ask God for His help. Then turn to page 170. Read Esther 7 and mark the following key words on your Observation Worksheet. Add any new words to your key-word bookmark.

king (King Ahasuerus) (color it orange)

Esther (queen, Queen Esther) (color it pink)

favor (color it yellow)

Haman (box it in black)

banquet (circle it in brown)

destroyed (killed, annihilated) (draw a black squiggly line like this: ~~~~~)

enemy (circle it in red)

anger (color it red)

Mordecai (color it blue)

Don't forget to mark the pronouns! And mark anything that tells you WHEN by drawing a 🕒 or green circle like this: ○ .

Now let's make a list on Esther's banquet.

Banquet #6

Esther 7:1 WHO gives the banquet?

_____

Esther 7:1 WHO is invited to the banquet?

_____

Esther 7:1 WHAT are they doing at the banquet?

_____

Esther 7:2 WHAT happens at the banquet? WHAT
does the king ask Esther?

_____

_____

Esther 7:2 WHEN does the king ask Esther about her
petition and request?

On the _____ _____

Esther 7:3 WHAT is Esther's petition and request?

"Let my _____ be _____ _____

as my _____, and my _____ as my

_____."

Esther 7:6 WHOM does Esther confront at the banquet?

_____

Can you imagine this scene? Haman is probably all relaxed and enjoying himself, feeling oh so important, when the king asks Esther a second time what her petition and request are. Esther shows courage and confidence as she reveals Haman as the enemy. Were you shocked?

Why don't you draw a picture of this incredible banquet?

Great artwork! Don't forget to practice your memory verse. This is Esther's petition and request to the king!

THE ENEMY IS REVEALED

"Are you guys ready to sleep in the Lincoln bedroom?" Uncle Matt asked as they walked inside the room. "This room was really Abraham Lincoln's office, and some of the furniture was his, but he never slept in this bed. Although," Uncle Matt changed his voice so that it sounded a little mysterious and spooky, "some visitors say when they sleep in here they sense Lincoln's ghost."

Molly jumped but then relaxed and smiled. "Oh, Uncle Matt! You know there aren't really ghosts!"

"I'm just saying what other people have reported who stayed in this room. You sure you want to sleep here?"

"We sure do!"

"Okay! I'm just messing with you. There is a legend about sensing Lincoln's ghost, but you are right. We don't have to worry about ghosts. You are two very blessed kids to get to stay in this room. It is rarely done. Why don't we go get a bedtime snack and find out what happens after Esther reveals Haman to the king?" Uncle Matt changed to his spooky, mysterious voice again, "HOW will the king react to what Haman has done? Will there be a turn of events?"

Don't forget to talk to God. Then turn to page 170. Read Esther 7 and ask the 5 W's and an H to solve the crossword puzzle on page 114.

> Esther 7:3 HOW did Esther ask the king? HOW did she present her request?
>
> 1. (Down) "If I have found _____ in your sight, O king, and if it
> 2. (Across) _____ the king"

> Esther 7:3 WHAT was Esther's request?
>
> 3. (Across) "Let my _____ be
> 4. (Down) _____ me as my petition, and my
> 5. (Across) _____ as my request."

> Esther 7:4 WHAT does Esther tell the king about her people and herself?
>
> 6. (Down) We have been _____ to be
> 7. (Down) _____, to be
> 8. (Across) _____, and to be
> 9. (Across) _____.

Esther 7:4 WHAT would Esther have done if they had only been sold as slaves?

    10. (Down) "I would have remained _____."

Esther 7:4 WHY would she have remained silent?

    11. (Across) Because the _____ would not be commensurate with the annoyance to the king

Esther 7:5 HOW does King Ahasuerus respond?

    12. (Down) "_____ is he, and where is he, who would presume to do thus?"

Esther 7:6 WHAT is Esther's response?

    13. (Across) "A foe and an _____ is this wicked

    14. (Across) _____."

Esther 7:6 HOW does Haman respond when he is revealed?

    15. (Down) He is _____.

Esther 7:7 HOW does the king respond to Esther's answer?

    16. (Down) He arose in his _____ from drinking wine and went into the palace garden.

Esther 7:7 WHAT did Haman do?

    17. (Down) He stayed to _____ for his life from Queen Esther.

Esther 7:7 WHAT did Haman see the king has determined against him?

   18. (Across) _____

Esther 7:8 WHAT did the king think when he returned from the palace garden and saw Haman falling on the couch where Esther was?

   19. (Down) "Will he even _____

     the queen with me in the house?"

Esther 7:8 When the king said this, WHAT do they do?

   20. (Across) They covered Haman's

   _____

Esther 7:9 WHAT does Harbonah tell the king?

   21. (Across) "Behold indeed, the _____

     standing at Haman's house fifty cubits high,

     which Haman made for

   22. (Down) _____."

Esther 7:9 WHAT does Harbonah say about Mordecai?

   23. (Across) He spoke _____ on behalf of

     the king.

Esther 7:9 WHAT did the king tell them to do to Haman?

   24. (Down) "_____ him on it."

Esther 7:10 WHAT did they do?

25. (Down) They _____ Haman on the

gallows which he had

26. (Across) _____ for Mordecai.

What a turn of events! Haman built these gallows 50 cubits high. That's 75 feet high! Haman didn't want anyone to miss seeing the hanging of Mordecai. But with a quick turn of events, Haman, the highest authority in Susa except for the king, will hang on the gallows he had built for Mordecai, his enemy.

Never forget that God takes action to rescue His people. God's timing is perfect. He is never early. He is never late. He does what He pleases in His perfect time and in His perfect plan. We must seek God, and then step out in faith and trust that He will work everything out in His perfect timing and plan!

As we wrap up this exciting week in the kingdom of the Medes and the Persians, let's do a little application of what we have learned. Let's look at some of Mordecai and Esther's character traits and apply them to our lives.

Character Trait #1: Faith.
Mordecai and Esther have faith.

Faith is believing God; it is taking Him at His Word. Faith is when you believe what God says in the Bible, and it shows in your actions. You decide to do what God says is right.

Mordecai and Esther know God's Word. They trust God. They sought Him by fasting for three days to prepare Esther to go before the king. They chose to trust God in a very scary and difficult situation.

Do you have faith? Have you put your trust in Jesus Christ?

    _X_ Yes   ____ No

Do you do what God says is right?

    ____ Yes   _X_ No

Do you want to please God?

    _X_ Yes   ____ No

Name one thing you do that shows you do what God says is right, and that you love, trust, and want to please God.

Make your faith strong by reading God's Word, memorizing it, and praying every day.

Character Trait #2: Courage
Mordecai and Esther have courage.

Courage is boldness; it is taking a stand and doing what you know is right, even though you are afraid.

Mordecai took a stand. He would not bow to Haman, God's enemy. He risked his life. He did not compromise what he believed.

Esther had courage. She went in to see the king, knowing that if he did not extend the golden scepter, she would be killed. And she pointed out her enemy to the king.

Do you have courage? Do you know someone who is being bullied? Will you be brave like Mordecai and Esther and stand up for what is right by telling someone and getting help for the one who is being bullied? Even if it means you will not be cool or popular or that the bully might turn on you? Write out one way you will have courage.

_____

What will you do when someone tries to get you to do the wrong thing?

_____

_____

_____

Character Trait #3: Humility
Mordecai and Esther have humility.

Humility is lack of pride. Humility is knowing our weaknesses as well as our strengths. It is submitting to God.

Mordecai tore his clothes and put on sackcloth and ashes. He wailed loudly and bitterly and fasted for Esther. Mordecai humbled himself before God.

Esther humbled herself by submitting to Mordecai's authority and doing what he told her to do. Esther humbled herself before God by fasting and seeking Him for three days. And look at how Esther approached the king. She made her request with humility, respect, and patience. She asks the king if she has his favor and has pleased him. You never see Esther or Mordecai show pride, even when they confront their enemy.

Are you humble? Do you submit yourself to those in authority over you?

_____ Yes _____ No

Are you respectful? How do you treat your parents and your teachers?

_____

_____

_____

_____

How do you talk about them to your friends when the adults aren't around to hear you?

_____

_____

_____

_____

Character Trait #4: Wisdom
Mordecai and Esther have wisdom.

To be wise is to show good judgment. It is to receive instruction, to be informed, to have knowledge and understanding, to have insight. A wise person listens to wise counsel.

Mordecai shows wisdom in knowing God's Word and God's

promises for His people, the Jews. He gives Esther wise advice on why God placed her in this royal position at this time in history.

Esther shows wisdom in listening to those in authority over her. She follows Hegai's advice about what to bring into the king's presence and obeys the wise counsel of Mordecai. Esther has a teachable heart. She also shows wisdom in the way she presents her request to the king.

Are you wise? Are you growing in knowledge? Do you study God's Word so you know the right thing to do?

_____ Yes   _____ No   _____ Sometimes

Are you teachable? Do you receive instruction from your parents and God's Word? Or do you refuse to listen and insist on doing it your way? Write out what you usually do.

_____

_____

_____

Character Trait #5: Self-discipline
Mordecai and Esther have self-discipline.

Self-discipline is learning to train and control your behavior. It is being able to turn away from temptation. It is choosing to do what is right, even when it is hard and difficult. It is sticking with something, even when it is dull and boring. It requires determination and sacrifice.

Mordecai shows self-discipline in his response to why he will not bow down to Haman. He simply says he is a Jew. He also shows self-discipline in the way he responds to his enemy and in fasting for three days.

Esther shows self-discipline when she fasts before going to see the king and waits patiently for the right time to tell the king what Haman has done. She controls her behavior. She chooses to do what is right, even though it is hard and difficult.

Do you have self-discipline? Do you know how to control your temper and your tongue?

_____ Yes _____ No _____ Sometimes

Do you know how to wait for something you want, or do you have to have it right now? Write out what you usually do.

_____

_____

_____

How can you develop self-discipline?

- Do something difficult every day.
- Learn to play a musical instrument, participate in a sport, or memorize Scripture. Practice every day. Don't give up or quit, even when it gets hard or boring.
- Save your money for something you want instead of asking your mom or dad to buy it for you.
- Do your homework or clean your room without your parents asking you to do it and without any grumbling or complaining.

You have done an excellent job! Now find a grown-up and say your memory verse out loud. We are so proud of you!

5

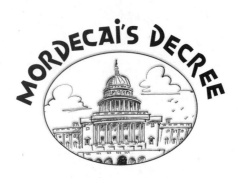

MORDECAI'S DECREE

ESTHER 8—10

Did you have a great time at the White House last week? We had a very special evening with the president of the United States, the first lady, and the president of Kenya. And we enjoyed the president's pups, Kate and Sadie.

We also watched a major event unfold in the kingdom of the Medes and Persians. Esther finds favor when she comes before the king.

As we continued our study, we saw the king spend a very sleepless night while Haman builds gallows and comes to the palace to ask the king about hanging Mordecai.

Were you surprised when Mordecai was rewarded for saving the king's life? God's timing is amazing! After Mordecai is honored, Haman runs home in mourning until the king's eunuchs escort him to Esther's banquet. Haman is revealed as the enemy and hanged on the gallows he built for Mordecai.

WHAT will happen next? Haman is gone, but there is still a decree to kill the Jews. HOW will God rescue His people from this horrible edict? Let's find out.

A CHANGE OF POWER

"Well, guys," Uncle Matt said, "this is your last week in Washington, D.C."

Molly replied, "I can't believe it. We have had the *best* time! We have a great form of government. I pray it never changes. We have learned so much, Uncle Matt. Thank you for all you've done!"

"Especially," Max added, "getting us in to meet the president, the first lady, the president of Kenya, and Kate and Sadie—that was incredible!"

When Sam heard Kate and Sadie's names, he looked up and barked his agreement.

Uncle Matt laughed at Sam before agreeing with Molly and Max. "It was great! Now we have one more branch of the government to learn about: the judicial branch. Max, why don't you tell us what you know about the judicial branch of our government?"

"The judicial branch of the government is all about laws. It makes sure that both the president and Congress follow the laws and decides if any laws have been broken. And it makes sure that state and federal laws agree with the Constitution. The judicial branch of the government includes the federal court system and the Supreme Court."

"That's great, Max! Now that we know about the judicial branch of our government, let's head back to Esther to find out the king's solution to the decree Haman made that can't be changed. Molly, why don't you pray for us?"

Now that we have prayed, turn to page 171. Read Esther 8:1-8 and mark the following key words on your Observation Worksheet. Add any new words to your key-word bookmark.

King Ahasuerus (king) (color it orange)

Queen Esther (queen, Esther) (color it pink)

Mordecai (color it blue)

Haman (Haman, the son of Hammedatha the Agagite) (box it in black)

Jew (draw a blue Star of David like this: ✡)

favor (color it yellow)

destroy (destruction) (draw a black squiggly line like this: ⌇⌇⌇⌇)

decree (box it in purple)

Don't forget to mark the pronouns! And mark anything that tells you WHEN by drawing a 🕐 or green circle like this: ◯ .

Esther 8:1 WHEN is this happening?

_____

_____

(This is the same day of Esther's banquet when Haman was hanged.)

Esther 8:1 WHAT does Esther tell the king?

_____

_____

The king now knows that Esther is Mordecai's cousin.

Esther 8:1 WHAT does King Ahasuerus give Queen Esther and Mordecai?

_____

_____

Ester 8:2 WHAT does the king give Mordecai?

_____

_____

Think about what you learned about the king's signet ring on page 67. WHY would the king give his signet ring to Mordecai?

_____

Esther 8:3 WHAT is Esther doing?

_____

_____

_____

_____

Esther 8:5 WHAT does Esther want the king to do?

"Let it be _____ to _____ the
_____ devised by Haman, the son of
Hammedatha the Agagite, which he wrote to
_____ the _____ who are in all
the king's provinces."

Esther 8:6 WHAT does Esther tell the king?

"How can I _____ to see the _____
which will befall my _____, and how can
I _____ to see the _____ of my
_____?"

Esther 8:7 WHAT does the king tell Esther and Mordecai?

_____

_____

Esther 8:8 WHAT is the king's solution to the decree that was made under Haman's authority?

"W __ __ __ __ to the _____ as you see fit in

the king's _____, and _____ it with the

_____ _____ _____."

Esther 8:8 WHAT do we learn about a decree?

_____

_____

What a change of events to see the king give his signet ring to Mordecai, giving him a position of power and authority. But instead of a celebration, we see Esther falling at the king's feet weeping and imploring the king to put an end to Haman's evil scheme to destroy her people.

According to the laws of the Medes and Persians, a decree that is written in the name of the king and sealed with the king's ring cannot be changed. WHAT is the king's solution? He tells Mordecai to write a decree, seal it with his ring, and send it to the Jews. WHAT will this decree say? And HOW can this decree keep the Jews from being destroyed? We'll find out tomorrow as we continue our research in Esther 8.

As we walk by the Washington Monument, let's solve this week's memory verse. Look at the Washington Monument puzzle and find the correct path through the maze by beginning at "Start."

After you find the correct path, fill in the blanks on page 126 with the correct words from the maze. Then look at Esther 10, find the reference for this verse, and fill in the blank. Practice saying this verse out loud three times in a row, three times every day this week!

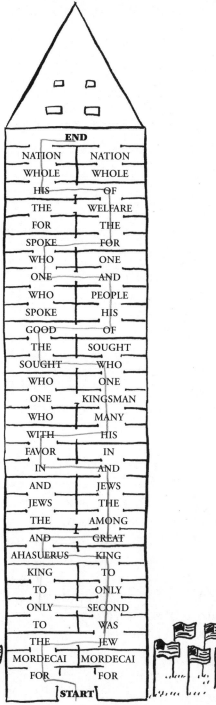

END

NATION	NATION
WHOLE	WHOLE
HIS	OF
THE	WELFARE
FOR	THE
SPOKE	FOR
WHO	ONE
ONE	AND
WHO	PEOPLE
SPOKE	HIS
GOOD	OF
THE	SOUGHT
SOUGHT	WHO
WHO	ONE
ONE	KINGSMAN
WHO	MANY
WITH	HIS
FAVOR	IN
IN	AND
AND	JEWS
JEWS	THE
THE	AMONG
AND	GREAT
AHASUERUS	KING
KING	TO
TO	ONLY
ONLY	SECOND
TO	WAS
THE	JEW
MORDECAI	MORDECAI
FOR	FOR

START

"_____ _____ _____ _____ _____

_____ _____ _____ _____

_____, _____ _____ _____

_____ _____ _____ _____ _____

_____ _____ _____, _____ _____

_____ _____ _____ _____ _____

_____ _____ _____ _____ _____

_____ _____ _____ _____ _____ _____

_____."

Esther 10:_____

Good job!

A Look at the Decrees

"Here we are," Uncle Matt said as they walked up the steps of the Supreme Court building. "Yesterday, Max told us about our third branch of our government—the judicial branch. Molly, why don't you tell us about the Supreme Court?"

"Okay, Uncle Matt. The Supreme Court is the highest court in the land. Its most important job is to interpret the U.S. Constitution. The Supreme Court has to decide how the rules in the Constitution apply today. The Supreme Court hears cases that are appealed from the lower courts.

"An appeal happens when a person in a trial objects to a verdict in a lower court. He or she asks a higher court to review the case to make sure the law was followed correctly. An appeal can reach the Supreme Court when there is a reason to believe the Constitution has been violated. Only the most important cases go to the Supreme Court."

"And," Max added, "there are no juries in the Supreme Court. It has nine judges, called 'justices,' who hear each case. Each of the justices are appointed by the president and must be approved by the Senate.

"First the judges listen to a case. Then they discuss it and vote. It takes fives votes—a majority—to decide a case. Once a decision is made by the Supreme Court, it can only be changed by another Supreme Court decision or by changing the Constitution."

"Very good, you guys! Now think about what is happening in Esther 8. A decree has been written in the name of the king and sealed with the king's ring. Esther is appealing to the king to save her people. She cannot bear the thought of her people being killed. But we know the decree can't be changed, according to the laws of the Medes and Persians. So the king tells Mordecai to write another decree.

"Okay, kids, today we get to find out about this second decree and HOW it can keep the Jews from being destroyed. Let's talk to God so we can get started."

Turn to page 172. Read Esther 8:9-17 and mark the following key words on your Observation Worksheet. Add any new words to your key-word bookmark.

King Ahasuerus (king) (color it orange)

Mordecai (color it blue)

Jew (draw a blue Star of David like this: ✡)

destroy (kill, annihilated) (draw a black squiggly line like this: ∿∿∿∿∿)

enemy (circle it in red)

decree (edict) (box it in purple)

Don't forget to mark the pronouns! And mark anything that tells you WHERE by double-underlining the <u><u>WHERE</u></u> in green. Mark anything that tells you WHEN by drawing a 🕒 or green circle like this: ○ .

Now get the facts. Ask those 5 W's and an H.

Esther 8:9 WHEN are the king's scribes called and this decree written?

In the _____ month which is _____, on

the _____-_____ day

Esther 8:10 WHAT did Mordecai do after he wrote in the king's name and sealed it with the king's signet ring?

_____

Let's look at the first edict in Esther 3:8-13 again. Read your Observation Worksheet on page 165 and then fill in the blanks about the first edict.

First Edict Under Haman

Esther 3:8-13 WHAT is the first edict that Haman commanded?

_____

Esther 3:13 WHEN would the Jews be destroyed?

On the _____ day of the _____

month, which is _____

Look at the second edict in Esther 8 on page 172 and fill in the blanks for the second edict.

Second Edict Under Mordecai

Esther 8:11 WHAT is the second edict? WHAT did the king grant the Jews?

_____

_____

Esther 8:12 WHEN would the Jews be allowed to defend their lives?

On the _____ day of the _____

month, the month of _____

Esther 8:13 WHAT else do we see about this second edict?

_____

WHY was it to be published? _____

_____

Esther 8:14 WHERE was the decree given out?

_____

Isn't that great? The first edict can't be revoked, so the king tells Mordecai to make another edict that allows the Jews to defend themselves and to destroy those who try to kill them on the day the first edict will be executed. *Execute* means to carry out, to perform.

HOW long do the Jews have from WHEN Mordecai's edict is made until the first edict is executed (carried out)? Look at Esther 8:12 to find out when the decree will be executed. Write it down on the first line.

Now look at Esther 8:9 to find out when Mordecai's decree was made. Write it down on the second line.

Subtract the month in Esther 8:9 from the month in Esther 8:12 to find out how long the Jews have to prepare before the first decree is carried out.

_____ month (Esther 8:12—the month the decree will be executed)

- _____ month (Esther 8:9—the month Mordecai's decree is made)

= _____ months to prepare

Esther 8:15 WHAT do we see about Mordecai?

_____

_____

Esther 8:15 WHAT did the city of Susa do?

_____

_____

Esther 8:17 WHAT was there in every city when the king's commandment and decree arrived?

_____

_____

Esther 8:17 WHAT do we see about the people of the land?

_____

_____

Esther 8:17 WHY?_____

_____

Fantastic! Finally, joy and gladness come to the Jews!

Don't forget to practice your memory verse. Tomorrow we will find out WHAT happens on the day the edicts are to be executed. HOW will this day of destruction turn out?

DAY THREE

THE EDICTS ARE EXECUTED

"Now that we have learned about the United States government, Uncle Matt is going to take us to the FBI, the Federal Bureau of Investigation," Max told Molly.

"The FBI's mission is 'to protect and defend the United States against terrorist and foreign intelligence threats and to enforce the criminal laws of the United States.' How neat is that? But before we meet the people who protect and defend the USA, let's head back to Esther and find out what happens next," Uncle Max said.

Ask God for His help. Then turn to page 173. Read Esther 9:1-16 and mark the following key words on your Observation Worksheet. Add any new words to your key-word bookmark.

King Ahasuerus (king) (color it orange)

edict (box it in purple)

Queen Esther (Esther) (color it pink)

Mordecai (color it blue)

Jew (draw a blue Star of David like this: ✡)

enemies (circle it in red)

hated (draw a black heart and put a zigzag line in the middle like this: ♡)

dread (color it green)

Haman (Haman, the son of Hammedatha the Agagite) (box it in black)

destroying (destroyed, killing, killed, kill) (draw a black squiggly line like this: 〜〜〜)

but they did not lay their hands on the plunder (under-line this key phrase in brown)

Don't forget to mark the pronouns! And mark anything that tells you WHERE by double-underlining the WHERE in green. Mark anything that tells you WHEN by drawing a green clock 🕐 or green circle like this: ○ .

Do your research. Ask the 5 W's and an H.

Esther 9:1 WHEN is the king's first command and edict going to be executed?

In the _____ month, _____, on

the _____ day

Esther 9:1 WHAT did the enemies of the Jews want to do?

_____

_____

Esther 9:1 WHAT happened?

_____

_____

Esther 9:2 WHAT did the Jews do?

_____

_____

Esther 9:3 WHY did all the princes of the provinces, the satraps, the governors, and those who were doing the king's business assist the Jews?

_____

_____

Esther 9:4 WHAT do we learn about Mordecai?

_____

_____

Esther 9:5 WHAT did the Jews do?

_____

_____

Esther 9:5 HOW are their enemies described?

   They h __ __ __ __ the Jews.

Esther 9:6 HOW many did the Jews kill at the citadel in Susa?

_____

_____

Esther 9:10 WHO are included in the men that are killed?

_____

_____

Esther 9:10 WHAT did the Jews not lay their hands on?

_____

_____

Esther 9:12-13 WHAT does the king ask Esther?

_____

_____

Esther 9:13 WHAT was Esther's request?

_____

_____

Esther 9:14 WHAT did the king do?

_____

Esther 9:15 WHAT other day did the Jews who were in Susa assemble?

On the _____ day of the month

_____

Esther 9:15 HOW many men did the Jews kill in Susa?

_____

_____

Esther 9:15 WHAT didn't they lay their hands on?

_____

_____

Esther 9:16 HOW many did the Jews who were in the king's provinces kill?

_____

_____

Esther 9:16 Did they lay their hands on the plunder?

_____

_____

Wow! Did you notice that as the Jews fought to defend themselves they only killed those who were their enemies, those who hated them, and they did not touch any of the belongings of their enemies?

Look at all the men who were killed because they hated the Jews and wanted to get rid of them. How very sad. But look at how much God loves the Jews. He did not allow their enemies to wipe them out. He protected them through Mordecai's edict.

Has there been a time in your life when something bad happened and God helped you? If there was, write out what happened on the following lines.

_____

_____

_____

Remember, God is right there with you! He provided a way to help the Jews, His chosen people, and He will help you!

Don't forget to practice your memory verse. Tomorrow we will find out what happens when the fighting is over.

DELIVERANCE AND CELEBRATION

"Hey, Uncle Matt!" Max said as they were eating breakfast. "How are we going to celebrate the Fourth of July today?"

"Ah, just wait. We are going to have a great time! Washington is a really terrific place to celebrate all kinds of festivals and holidays because a lot of the celebrations are held to remember special days in American history, such as the Fourth of July. The Fourth of July is a special day for Americans to remember when the United States announced their independence from Great Britain in 1776.

"But before we begin our special celebration, we need to head back in history and find out what happens now that the Jews have defended their people and nation. Do they celebrate their victory?"

Don't forget to pray! Then turn to page 174. Read Esther 9:17-32 and mark the following key words on your Observation Worksheet. Add any new words to your key-word bookmark.

King Ahasuerus (king) (color it orange)

Queen Esther (Esther) (color it pink)

Mordecai (color it blue)

Jew (draw a blue Star of David like this: ✡)

enemies (circle it in red)

mourning (circle it in red and color it black)

Haman (Haman, the son of Hammedatha the Agagite) (box it in black)

destroy (draw a black squiggly line like this: ∿∿∿)

Pur (Purim) (box it in orange) (Also, turn to page 164 and mark *Pur* in Esther 3:7)

Don't forget to mark the pronouns! And mark anything that tells you WHERE by double-underlining the WHERE in green. Mark anything that tells you WHEN by drawing a green clock ⏰ or green circle like this: ◯ .

Now ask those 5 W's and an H.

Esther 9:16-17 WHEN did the Jews in the king's provinces kill the 75,000 men?

On the _____ day of the month of

_____

Esther 9:17 WHAT did they do on the fourteenth day?

_____

_____

Esther 9:18 WHAT days did the Jews in Susa assemble on?

The _____ and _____ day of
the same month

Esther 9:18 WHEN did the Jews in Susa rest, feast, and rejoice?

On the _____ day of the month

Esther 9:19 WHAT did the Jews do in the rural areas?

_____

_____

Esther 9:20 WHAT did Mordecai do?

_____

_____

Esther 9:21 WHAT did Mordecai oblige them to do?

_____

_____

Esther 9:22 WHY were the Jews to celebrate?

_____

_____

Esther 9:22 HOW were they to celebrate?

_____

Esther 9:24 WHAT had Haman cast to decide when to destroy the Jews?

_____, that is the _____

Esther 9:26 WHAT did they call these days of celebration? _____

WHY? _____

Esther 9:27 WHAT were the Jews to establish as a custom?

_____

_____

Esther 9:27 WHEN were they to celebrate?

_____

_____

Esther 9:27 WHO was to celebrate?

The _____, their _____, and all those who _____ themselves with them

Esther 9:28 WHAT do we see about these days of Purim?

_____

_____

Esther 9:28 WHY were they to continue to celebrate the days of Purim?

So it would not f _ _ _ from their m _ _ _ _ _ _

Esther 9:29 WHAT did Queen Esther and Mordecai do?

_____

_____

Esther 9:30 WHERE did Mordecai send these letters?

_____

_____

Esther 9:30 WHAT were the words of these letters?

_____

_____

_____

Esther 9:31 WHAT were they to establish?

_____

_____

Esther 9:32 WHOSE command established these customs for Purim?

_____

_____

Esther 9:32 WHERE was this command written?

_____

_____

Pretty cool, huh? Look at how the Jews took Pur, the casting of the lot that Haman used to decide when to destroy them, and turned it into Purim, a holiday to celebrate their deliverance! This special holiday is to remind the Jews of God's great victory. He always triumphs! It is a day of feasting and rejoicing. The Jews have gone from great sorrow to gladness. It is a time to rest, feast, and rejoice.

Isn't it *awesome* that the Jews celebrate this holiday every year so they won't forget how God rescued them from their enemies? HOW do the Jewish people celebrate Purim today? Look at what Max and Molly found out in their research.

Let's Celebrate Purim

Purim is celebrated on the fourteenth day of Adar, which is usually in March.

Before Purim begins, there is a fast that is called the "fast of Esther," to represent when she fasted for three days before she went to see the king.

Then Jews listen to the book of Esther as it is read. The book of Esther is known as the *Megillah,* which means "scroll." The Megillah is read in the evening and in the morning on Purim day. (That's where the expression "the whole Megillah" comes from.)

As the scroll is read, anytime Haman's name is read, the people hiss, stamp their feet, and use noisemakers. This is done to blot out the name of Haman. When Mordecai's name is read, the people cheer.

Jews send gifts of at least two kinds of food, such as candies, cookies, fruit, or bottles of juice, to at least one person to show gratitude for their friendship.

They also give to at least two needy people, or if they don't know someone who is needy, they give to a charitable organization.

Jews have a festive meal on Purim afternoon. They eat and rejoice with family and friends and sing Jewish songs to have fun and share happiness.

They thank God.

Some people also celebrate with dancing, dressing up in costumes, and putting on plays.

Doesn't that sound like fun? Maybe you can have your own Purim festival. You and your family can read the book of Esther, hissing and booing against Haman and cheering for Mordecai. And you could also make a special treat to eat called Purim Hamantashen. Here's the recipe.

Purim Hamantashen

Ingredients

4 eggs

1 cup of sugar

½ cup oil

1 tablespoon lemon juice and lemon rind from half a lemon

1 teaspoon vanilla

5 cups sifted flour

2 teaspoons baking powder

jelly for the filling

1 beaten egg to brush the cookies with

Directions

Preheat oven to 350°F.

Beat eggs and sugar. Add the oil, lemon juice, lemon rind, vanilla, flour, and baking powder.

Divide the dough into four parts. Stretch it about an inch thick on a floured surface and cut out circles with a cup.

Put ½ teaspoon of jelly in the middle of each circle.

Lift the right and left side of each circle and put them together in the middle on top of the jelly, forming a triangle. Lift the third side to the center and press it together with the first two.

Put the cookies on a greased pan. Brush with the beaten egg.

Bake for 20 minutes.*

You can also share some food gifts with your friends, give to a charity, sing songs, and thank God for all He has done for you. Have a great time!

Can you think of an occasion that Christians celebrate that starts out with sorrow and ends up with rejoicing?

_ _ _ _ _ _!

Did you guess? It's Easter. We are sad on Friday because Jesus died on the cross to pay for our sins, but on Sunday we celebrate because He was resurrected. He didn't stay dead! He lives forever! We get dressed up in new clothes or very nice clothes to show that we are new creations in Christ. We go to church to worship God, eat a great lunch, and spend time with friends and family to celebrate that Jesus died to save us! How wonderful is that?

And guess what? One day very soon Jesus will come back to reign on this earth. Oh, what a day of *celebration* that will be! Are you ready for that *awesome* day?

Don't forget to practice your memory verse.

A TRIBUTE FROM THE KING

"Sam, stop! Come back here, boy! You are going to get lost!" Max yelled as Sam took off across the National Mall.

"I think he wants to be the first one to see the Lincoln Memorial," Molly said, panting as she helped Max chase Sam.

Uncle Matt put his fingers in his mouth and gave a loud whistle.

Sam immediately turned around and headed straight for Max, knocking him down. Molly fell beside them laughing.

"Sam, you are one bad dog—and on our last day in D.C. Bad, bad dog!"

Uncle Matt overheard Max scolding Sam when he caught up with the kids. "Well, Max, you do have to admit he's been pretty good so far on our Washington adventure."

"Except," Molly added, "when he ran through the Rose Garden at the White House."

Max jumped in. "That's only because he was following Kate and Sadie, the president's pups. And," Max added, "he didn't give the president a face-licking."

"Only because you had a death grip on him," Molly answered. "You almost squeezed him to death trying to keep him in your arms when we were in the Oval Office."

Uncle Matt and Max laughed.

"Okay," Uncle Matt said, "let's put Sam on his leash and catch our breath by sitting down before we go inside the Lincoln Memorial. The Lincoln Memorial is one of the United States' symbols of freedom. Abraham Lincoln was the sixteenth president of the United States. His second inaugural speech and his Gettysburg Address are engraved on the interior walls of the building."

Max asked, "Isn't this also where Dr. Martin Luther King, Jr., gave his 'I have a dream' speech for equal rights for all Americans?"

"It sure is," Uncle Matt replied. "Since we're resting, let's finish our study in Esther. First we'll talk to God and thank Him for all our freedoms and ask for His help as we study."

All right! Now that we have prayed, it's time to find out what happens after the Jews celebrate Purim. But before we do, let's take a look back at Esther 9. Turn to page 173 and read Esther 9:5-14.

Esther 9:6-10 WHAT happens to Haman's sons?

_____

Esther 9:13 WHAT does Esther ask the king?

_____

Think about this for a minute. Haman's sons were killed, according to verses 6-10, so WHY does Esther want the king to make an edict and hang them on the gallows after they are dead?

Do you know that *gallows* literally means "tree" in Hebrew? Now look up and read Deuteronomy 21:22-23 in your Bible.

Deuteronomy 21:22 WHAT did they do to a man who committed a sin worthy of death?

_____

Deuteronomy 21:23 WHAT do we see about the person who is hanged on a tree?

He is _____ of God.

Esther wanted to show that Haman's sons, the enemies of the Jews, were cursed.

Look up and read Galatians 3:13-14 in your Bible.

WHAT is everyone who hangs on a tree?

_____

WHO redeemed us from the curse of the law?

_____

WHO became a curse for us?_____

There's our hope: Jesus! We are cursed because we are all sinners. And sin leads to death, so we all deserve to die. But because death would separate us from God forever, God in His love and mercy sent His only Son, Jesus Christ, to die on a cross, to take away our sins and reconcile us (make things right) with

God so we could have eternal life. God gives us a free gift that we don't deserve.

Yesterday we talked about celebrating Easter and how Jesus would come back one day to reign on the earth. Are you ready to celebrate with Jesus? Have you accepted the *incredible* gift of salvation from God?

____ Yes   ____ No

If you haven't and you want to, the first thing you need to know is WHO Jesus is and believe it. You have to believe that Jesus is God's Son, that He is God, that He came to earth as a man, that as a man He lived a perfect life without sin, and that He died on a cross to pay for your sins. Then He was buried and God raised Him three days later from the dead. Jesus is the *only* Savior!

You have to believe you are a sinner, and that you need someone to save you because you can't save yourself. You have to be willing to confess you are a sinner to God and turn away from your sin (repent). You have to be willing to turn your entire life over to God to become a follower of Jesus Christ.

To believe in Jesus means you are willing to turn away from doing things your way and to obey Jesus. You want Jesus to have complete control over your life.

Take some time and think about what you have learned about who Jesus is and WHAT He has done for you. Ask yourself, "Am I ready to give my life to Jesus and let Him take over my life?"

It's a big decision, so really think about it. If you aren't sure you understand, you can talk to a grown-up who is a Christian, who believes in Jesus. When you are ready, ask a grown-up to help you take that step. You can pray like this:

Thank You, God, for loving me and sending Your Son, Jesus Christ, to die for my sins. I am sorry for the things I have done wrong. I repent—I know sin is wrong and I don't want to do things my way anymore. I want to receive Jesus Christ as my Savior. I turn my entire life over to You! Amen.

Once you have turned your life over to Jesus, He will give you the gift of the Holy Spirit to live inside you and give you power to live for God. How amazing is that!

All right! Let's find out what happens after Purim as we wrap up our "H-i-s S-t-o-r-y" adventure. Turn to page 176. Read Esther 10 and mark these key words on your Observation Worksheet.

King Ahasuerus (king) (color it orange)

Mordecai (color it blue)

Jew (draw a blue Star of David like this: ✡)

favor (color it yellow)

Don't forget to mark the pronouns!

Let's find out how this story ends. Ask those 5 W's and an H.

Esther 10:1 WHAT did King Ahasuerus do?

He laid a _____ on the _____ and on the coastlands of the _____.

Esther 10:2 WHAT was this tribute about?

All the _____ of his _____ and _____, and the full account of the _____ of _____

Esther 10:2 WHERE were they written?

In the _____ of the _____ of the _____ of _____ and _____

Esther 10:2-3 WHAT do we learn about Mordecai?

The king _____ Mordecai. Mordecai

was _____ only to King Ahasuerus.

He was _____ among the _____

and in _____ with his many _____.

Mordecai sought the _____ of his

_____ and he _____ for the

_____ of his whole _____.

Now find the words from all of the blanks about Esther 10 on pages 148 and 149 and circle them in the word search. If a word is used more than once, you only have to find and circle it one time.

K	M	K	S	I	E	G	A	T	D	G	A	A	Z	K
J	Z	O	U	E	R	K	R	N	N	O	I	D	U	I
V	E	S	R	E	L	I	O	K	A	O	S	V	V	N
M	Y	W	A	D	B	C	O	P	L	D	R	A	E	S
N	T	T	S	U	E	O	I	U	S	S	E	N	C	M
E	I	K	T	S	B	C	X	N	S	F	P	C	S	E
J	R	E	N	A	S	T	A	E	O	U	X	E	Z	N
T	O	A	N	A	Y	P	N	I	K	R	Z	D	V	W
Q	H	O	F	V	T	T	Y	P	J	Y	H	U	C	S
O	T	I	C	L	A	I	R	O	V	A	F	C	E	M
G	U	K	E	E	E	N	O	I	G	R	H	A	K	E
F	A	J	R	S	Y	W	I	N	G	M	R	O	Q	D
O	Z	G	P	E	O	P	L	E	D	S	C	E	H	I
S	T	N	E	M	H	S	I	L	P	M	O	C	C	A
W	W	S	T	R	E	N	G	T	H	K	I	N	G	S

All right! How many heroes and/or heroines are

there in the book of Esther? _____

The name of the book is Esther, but we have discovered there is a Jew named Mordecai whom God used to lead and guide this young lady. From the beginning to the end, we have seen Mordecai show courage and wisdom. He never compromises. He rises to great position, but he never looks at the gain for himself. Instead, he sought the good of his people and spoke for the welfare of his nation. What an *awesome* man of God! Give Mordecai a cheer!

Esther was an amazing young lady. She submitted to Mordecai's authority, she humbled herself before God, and she approached the king with humility, respect, and patience. She had courage and wisdom. Esther trusted God in a very difficult and scary situation. She was willing to lay down her life for her nation.

If you are a girl, are you an Esther? _____

If you are a boy, are you a Mordecai? _____

Say your memory verse out loud to remind yourself of this woman and man of God who laid down their lives to be used by God to save their nation!

BACK AT THE NATIONAL MALL

You did it! You have finished a very important book in history. Way to go! We are so proud of you! Just look at all you have discovered. You opened the most important book in history—the Bible—and saw a Jewish girl growing up in the kingdom of the Medes and Persians. She is taken from her family and placed in a palace, where she may or may not be chosen to be the new queen. Esther doesn't have a choice about her life, but she never shows anger or bitterness over her circumstances.

How about you? How do you handle disappointments and hard situations?

Will you trust God to work everything "for your good" like Esther did?

You also found that God (even though He isn't mentioned specifically in the book of Esther) worked out His plan and His purpose in His perfect time as the events unfolded in Esther.

Esther becomes the new queen. And as she faces a crisis, you see her listen to the wise advice of Mordecai and seek God with fasting. Esther goes from being afraid to die to having courage. She surrenders her life to God and uses her position to save her people.

And you learned that Mordecai, an awesome man of God, knows who God is and lives out his faith. He is courageous. He will not bow to his enemies. He loves and cares for Esther, but he is willing to ask her to die for the good of their nation. Mordecai knows God's promises. Even when he is mourning, he knows God will deliver the Jews. Mordecai only does good for his people. *Wow!*

You have discovered so much in this very small book. What will you do with what you have learned? You may think, "But I am just a kid." But guess what? God has a plan for *you* in the future, but He also has a plan for you *right now*. He wants you to love Him, to turn your life over to Jesus Christ, to learn His Word, and to share His Word and Jesus with people.

Have you invited Jesus Christ into your life? Are you ready to love and serve God instead of making life all about *you* and what you want? Remember, a *celebration* is coming very soon! Jesus is coming!

As we wrap up our adventure in Washington, D.C., we pray that you will give God first place in your life, that you will become a leader for God and your nation. Always know that God is with you. He loves you! He is in control. He rules everything, including the nation! Be courageous and trust Him! Don't forget to go to www.precept.org/D4Ycertificate to print your special certificate for finishing this book.

We hope you'll join us for another adventure in God's Word real soon.

molly, Max, and

(Sam)

PUZZLE ANSWERS

Page 14

"For the queen's _conduct_ will become _known_ to all the _women_ causing them to look with _contempt_ on their _husbands_ by saying, King _Ahasuerus_ _commanded_ Queen _Vashti_ to be brought in to his _presence_, but she did not _come."_

Esther 1:17

Page 33

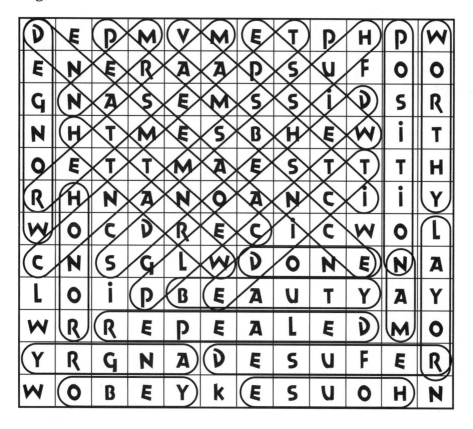

Page 39

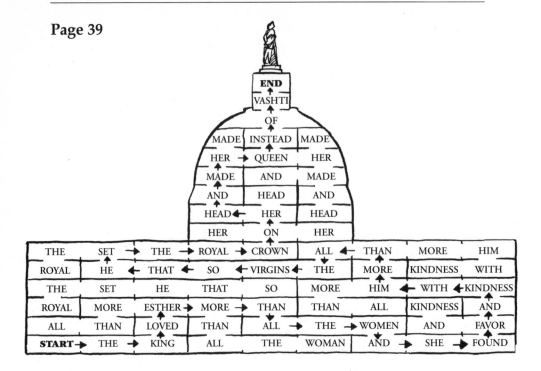

Page 40

"The king loved Esther more than all the women, and she found favor and kindness with him more than all the virgins, so that he set the royal crown on her head and made her queen instead of Vashti."

Esther 2:17

Page 47

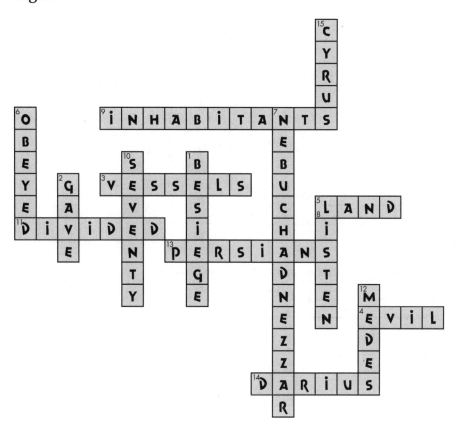

Page 63

"For if _you_ remain _silent_ at this _time, relief_ and _deliverance_ will _arise_ for the _Jews_ from another _place_ and you and your _father's house_ will _perish_. And who _knows_ whether _you_ have not _attained royalty_ for such a _time_ as this?"

Esther 4:14

Page 76

Page 94

"Then Queen Esther replied, 'If I have found favor in your sight, O king, and if it pleases the king, let my life be given me as my petition, and my people as my request."

Esther 7:3

Page 114

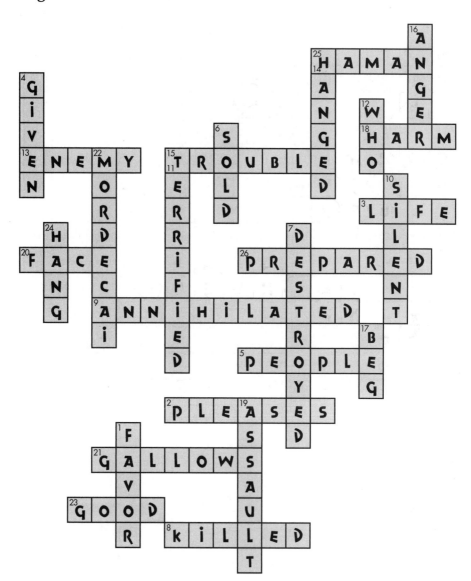

Bible ↙

125

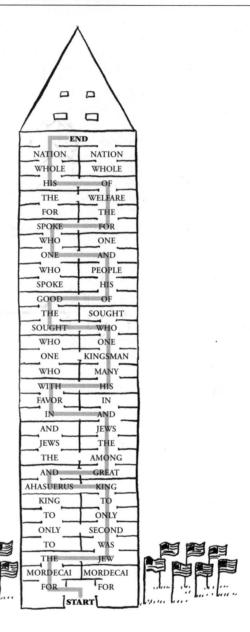

Page 126

"For Mordecai the Jew was second only to King Ahasuerus, and great among the Jews and in favor with his many kinsmen, one who sought the good of his people and one who spoke for the welfare of his whole nation."

Esther 10:3

Page 149

k	M	k	S	i	E	G	A	T	D	G	A	A	Z	k
j	Z	O	U	E	R	k	R	N	N	O	i	D	U	i
V	E	S	R	E	L	i	O	k	A	O	S	V	V	N
M	Y	W	A	D	B	C	O	P	L	D	R	A	E	S
N	T	T	S	U	E	O	i	U	S	S	E	N	C	M
E	j	k	T	S	B	C	x	N	S	F	P	C	S	E
j	R	E	N	A	S	T	A	E	O	U	x	E	Z	N
T	O	A	N	A	Y	P	N	i	k	R	Z	D	V	W
q	H	O	F	V	T	T	Y	P	j	Y	H	U	C	S
O	T	i	C	L	A	i	R	O	V	A	F	C	E	M
G	U	k	E	E	E	N	O	i	G	R	H	A	k	E
F	A	j	R	S	Y	W	i	N	G	M	R	O	q	D
O	Z	G	P	E	O	P	L	E	D	S	C	E	H	i
S	T	N	E	M	H	S	i	L	P	M	O	C	C	A
W	W	S	T	R	E	N	G	T	H	k	i	N	G	S

OBSERVATION WORKSHEETS

ESTHER

Chapter 1

1 Now it took place in the days of Ahasuerus, the Ahasuerus who reigned from India to Ethiopia over 127 provinces,

2 in those days as King Ahasuerus sat on his royal throne which was at the citadel in Susa,

3 in the third year of his reign he gave a banquet for all his princes and attendants, the army officers of Persia and Media, the nobles and the princes of his provinces being in his presence.

4 And he displayed the riches of his royal glory and the splendor of his great majesty for many days, 180 days.

5 When these days were completed, the king gave a banquet lasting seven days for all the people who were present at the citadel in Susa, from the greatest to the least, in the court of the garden of the king's palace.

6 There were hangings of fine white and violet linen held by cords of fine purple linen on silver rings and marble columns, and couches of gold and silver on a mosaic pavement of porphyry, marble, mother-of-pearl and precious stones.

7 Drinks were served in golden vessels of various kinds, and the royal wine was plentiful according to the king's bounty.

8 The drinking was done according to the law, there was no compulsion, for so the king had given orders to each official of his household that he should do according to the desires of each person.

9 Queen Vashti also gave a banquet for the women in the palace which belonged to King Ahasuerus.

10 On the seventh day, when the heart of the king was merry with wine, he commanded Mehuman, Biztha, Harbona, Bigtha, Abagtha, Zethar and Carkas, the seven eunuchs who served in the presence of King Ahasuerus,

11 to bring Queen Vashti before the king with her royal crown in order to display her beauty to the people and the princes, for she was beautiful.

12 But Queen Vashti refused to come at the king's command delivered by the eunuchs. Then the king became very angry and his wrath burned within him.

13 Then the king said to the wise men who understood the times—for it was the custom of the king so to speak before all who knew law and justice

14 and were close to him: Carshena, Shethar, Admatha, Tarshish, Meres, Marsena and Memucan, the seven princes of Persia and Media who had access to the king's presence and sat in the first place in the kingdom—

15 "According to law, what is to be done with Queen Vashti, because she did not obey the command of King Ahasuerus delivered by the eunuchs?"

16 In the presence of the king and the princes, Memucan said, "Queen Vashti has wronged not only the king but also all the princes and all the peoples who are in all the provinces of King Ahasuerus.

17 "For the queen's conduct will become known to all the women causing them to look with contempt on their husbands by saying, 'King Ahasuerus commanded Queen Vashti to be brought in to his presence, but she did not come.'

18 "This day the ladies of Persia and Media who have heard of the queen's conduct will speak in the same way to all the king's princes, and there will be plenty of contempt and anger.

19 "If it pleases the king, let a royal edict be issued by him and let it be written in the laws of Persia and Media so that it cannot be repealed, that Vashti may no longer come into the presence of King Ahasuerus, and let the king give her royal position to another who is more worthy than she.

20 "When the king's edict which he will make is heard throughout

2

kingdom, great as it is, then all women will give honor to their
ands, great and small."

This word pleased the king and the princes, and the king did as
Memucan proposed.

22 So he sent letters to all the king's provinces, to each province according to its script and to every people according to their language, that
every man should be the master in his own house and the one who
speaks in the language of his own people.

Chapter 2

1 After these things when the anger of King Ahasuerus had subsided,
he remembered Vashti and what she had done and what had been
decreed against her.

2 Then the king's attendants, who served him, said, "Let beautiful
young virgins be sought for the king.

3 "Let the king appoint overseers in all the provinces of his kingdom
that they may gather every beautiful young virgin to the citadel of Susa,
to the harem, into the custody of Hegai, the king's eunuch, who is in
charge of the women; and let their cosmetics be given them.

4 "Then let the young lady who pleases the king be queen in place
of Vashti." And the matter pleased the king, and he did accordingly.

5 Now there was at the citadel in Susa a Jew whose name was
Mordecai, the son of Jair, the son of Shimei, the son of Kish, a Benjamite,

6 who had been taken into exile from Jerusalem with the captives who
had been exiled with Jeconiah king of Judah, whom Nebuchadnezzar
the king of Babylon had exiled.

7 He was bringing up Hadassah, that is Esther, his uncle's daughter,
for she had no father or mother. Now the young lady was beautiful
of form and face, and when her father and her mother died, Mordecai
took her as his own daughter.

8 So it came about when the command and decree of the king were
heard and many young ladies were gathered to the citadel of Susa into

the custody of Hegai, that Esther was taken to the king's palace into the custody of Hegai, who was in charge of the women.

9 Now the young lady pleased him and found favor with him. So he quickly provided her with her cosmetics and food, gave her seven choice maids from the king's palace and transferred her and her maids to the best place in the harem.

10 Esther did not make known her people or her kindred, for Mordecai had instructed her that she should not make them known.

11 Every day Mordecai walked back and forth in front of the court of the harem to learn how Esther was and how she fared.

12 Now when the turn of each young lady came to go in to King Ahasuerus, after the end of her twelve months under the regulations for the women—for the days of their beautification were completed as follows: six months with oil of myrrh and six months with spices and the cosmetics for women—

13 the young lady would go in to the king in this way: anything that she desired was given her to take with her from the harem to the king's palace.

14 In the evening she would go in and in the morning she would return to the second harem, to the custody of Shaashgaz, the king's eunuch who was in charge of the concubines. She would not again go in to the king unless the king delighted in her and she was summoned by name.

15 Now when the turn of Esther, the daughter of Abihail the uncle of Mordecai who had taken her as his daughter, came to go in to the king, she did not request anything except what Hegai, the king's eunuch who was in charge of the women, advised. And Esther found favor in the eyes of all who saw her.

16 So Esther was taken to King Ahasuerus to his royal palace in the tenth month which is the month Tebeth, in the seventh year of his reign.

17 The king loved Esther more than all the women, and she found favor and kindness with him more than all the virgins, so that he set the royal crown on her head and made her queen instead of Vashti.

18 Then the king gave a great banquet, Esther's banquet, for all his princes and his servants; he also made a holiday for the provinces and gave gifts according to the king's bounty.

19 When the virgins were gathered together the second time, then Mordecai was sitting at the king's gate.

20 Esther had not yet made known her kindred or her people, even as Mordecai had commanded her; for Esther did what Mordecai told her as she had done when under his care.

21 In those days, while Mordecai was sitting at the king's gate, Bigthan and Teresh, two of the king's officials from those who guarded the door, became angry and sought to lay hands on King Ahasuerus.

22 But the plot became known to Mordecai and he told Queen Esther, and Esther informed the king in Mordecai's name.

23 Now when the plot was investigated and found to be so, they were both hanged on a gallows; and it was written in the Book of the Chronicles in the king's presence.

Chapter 3

1 After these events King Ahasuerus promoted Haman, the son of Hammedatha the Agagite, and advanced him and established his authority over all the princes who were with him.

2 All the king's servants who were at the king's gate bowed down and paid homage to Haman; for so the king had commanded concerning him. But Mordecai neither bowed down nor paid homage.

3 Then the king's servants who were at the king's gate said to Mordecai, "Why are you transgressing the king's command?"

4 Now it was when they had spoken daily to him and he would not listen to them, that they told Haman to see whether Mordecai's reason would stand; for he had told them that he was a Jew.

5 When Haman saw that Mordecai neither bowed down nor paid homage to him, Haman was filled with rage.

6 But he disdained to lay hands on Mordecai alone, for they had

told him who the people of Mordecai were; therefore Haman sought to destroy all the Jews, the people of Mordecai, who were throughout the whole kingdom of Ahasuerus.

7 In the first month, which is the month Nisan, in the twelfth year of King Ahasuerus, Pur, that is the lot, was cast before Haman from day to day and from month to month, until the twelfth month, that is the month Adar.

8 Then Haman said to King Ahasuerus, "There is a certain people scattered and dispersed among the peoples in all the provinces of your kingdom; their laws are different from those of all other people and they do not observe the king's laws, so it is not in the king's interest to let them remain.

9 "If it is pleasing to the king, let it be decreed that they be destroyed, and I will pay ten thousand talents of silver into the hands of those who carry on the king's business, to put into the king's treasuries."

10 Then the king took his signet ring from his hand and gave it to Haman, the son of Hammedatha the Agagite, the enemy of the Jews.

11 The king said to Haman, "The silver is yours, and the people also, to do with them as you please."

12 Then the king's scribes were summoned on the thirteenth day of the first month, and it was written just as Haman commanded to the king's satraps, to the governors who were over each province and to the princes of each people, each province according to its script, each people according to its language, being written in the name of King Ahasuerus and sealed with the king's signet ring.

13 Letters were sent by couriers to all the king's provinces to destroy, to kill and to annihilate all the Jews, both young and old, women and children, in one day, the thirteenth day of the twelfth month, which is the month Adar, and to seize their possessions as plunder.

14 A copy of the edict to be issued as law in every province was published to all the peoples so that they should be ready for this day.

15 The couriers went out impelled by the king's command while the

decree was issued at the citadel in Susa; and while the king and Haman
sat down to drink, the city of Susa was in confusion.

Chapter 4

1 When Mordecai learned all that had been done, he tore his clothes,
put on sackcloth and ashes, and went out into the midst of the city and
wailed loudly and bitterly.

2 He went as far as the king's gate, for no one was to enter the king's
gate clothed in sackcloth.

3 In each and every province where the command and decree of the
king came, there was great mourning among the Jews, with fasting,
weeping and wailing; and many lay on sackcloth and ashes.

4 Then Esther's maidens and her eunuchs came and told her, and
the queen writhed in great anguish. And she sent garments to clothe
Mordecai that he might remove his sackcloth from him, but he did not
accept them.

5 Then Esther summoned Hathach from the king's eunuchs, whom
the king had appointed to attend her, and ordered him to go to Mordecai
to learn what this was and why it was.

6 So Hathach went out to Mordecai to the city square in front of the
king's gate.

7 Mordecai told him all that had happened to him, and the exact
amount of money that Haman had promised to pay to the king's treasuries for the destruction of the Jews.

8 He also gave him a copy of the text of the edict which had been
issued in Susa for their destruction, that he might show Esther and
inform her, and to order her to go in to the king to implore his favor
and to plead with him for her people.

9 Hathach came back and related Mordecai's words to Esther.

10 Then Esther spoke to Hathach and ordered him to reply to Mordecai:

11 "All the king's servants and the people of the king's provinces know
that for any man or woman who comes to the king to the inner court

who is not summoned, he has but one law, that he be put to death, unless the king holds out to him the golden scepter so that he may live. And I have not been summoned to come to the king for these thirty days."

12 They related Esther's words to Mordecai.

13 Then Mordecai told them to reply to Esther, "Do not imagine that you in the king's palace can escape any more than all the Jews.

14 "For if you remain silent at this time, relief and deliverance will arise for the Jews from another place and you and your father's house will perish. And who knows whether you have not attained royalty for such a time as this?"

15 Then Esther told them to reply to Mordecai,

16 "Go, assemble all the Jews who are found in Susa, and fast for me; do not eat or drink for three days, night or day. I and my maidens also will fast in the same way. And thus I will go in to the king, which is not according to the law; and if I perish, I perish."

17 So Mordecai went away and did just as Esther had commanded him.

Chapter 5

1 Now it came about on the third day that Esther put on her royal robes and stood in the inner court of the king's palace in front of the king's rooms, and the king was sitting on his royal throne in the throne room, opposite the entrance to the palace.

2 When the king saw Esther the queen standing in the court, she obtained favor in his sight; and the king extended to Esther the golden scepter which was in his hand. So Esther came near and touched the top of the scepter.

3 Then the king said to her, "What is troubling you, Queen Esther? And what is your request? Even to half of the kingdom it shall be given to you."

4 Esther said, "If it pleases the king, may the king and Haman come this day to the banquet that I have prepared for him."

5 Then the king said, "Bring Haman quickly that we may do as Esther desires." So the king and Haman came to the banquet which Esther had prepared.

6 As they drank their wine at the banquet, the king said to Esther, "What is your petition, for it shall be granted to you. And what is your request? Even to half of the kingdom it shall be done."

7 So Esther replied, "My petition and my request is:

8 if I have found favor in the sight of the king, and if it pleases the king to grant my petition and do what I request, may the king and Haman come to the banquet which I will prepare for them, and tomorrow I will do as the king says."

9 Then Haman went out that day glad and pleased of heart; but when Haman saw Mordecai in the king's gate and that he did not stand up or tremble before him, Haman was filled with anger against Mordecai.

10 Haman controlled himself, however, went to his house and sent for his friends and his wife Zeresh.

11 Then Haman recounted to them the glory of his riches, and the number of his sons, and every instance where the king had magnified him and how he had promoted him above the princes and servants of the king.

12 Haman also said, "Even Esther the queen let no one but me come with the king to the banquet which she had prepared; and tomorrow also I am invited by her with the king.

13 "Yet all of this does not satisfy me every time I see Mordecai the Jew sitting at the king's gate."

14 Then Zeresh his wife and all his friends said to him, "Have a gallows fifty cubits high made and in the morning ask the king to have Mordecai hanged on it; then go joyfully with the king to the banquet." And the advice pleased Haman so he had the gallows made.

Chapter 6

1 During that night the king could not sleep so he gave an order to

bring the book of records, the chronicles, and they were read before the king.

2 It was found written what Mordecai had reported concerning Bigthana and Teresh, two of the king's eunuchs who were doorkeepers, that they had sought to lay hands on King Ahasuerus.

3 The king said, "What honor or dignity has been bestowed on Mordecai for this?" Then the king's servants who attended him said, "Nothing has been done for him."

4 So the king said, "Who is in the court?" Now Haman had just entered the outer court of the king's palace in order to speak to the king about hanging Mordecai on the gallows which he had prepared for him.

5 The king's servants said to him, "Behold, Haman is standing in the court." And the king said, "Let him come in."

6 So Haman came in and the king said to him, "What is to be done for the man whom the king desires to honor?" And Haman said to himself, "Whom would the king desire to honor more than me?"

7 Then Haman said to the king, "For the man whom the king desires to honor,

8 let them bring a royal robe which the king has worn, and the horse on which the king has ridden, and on whose head a royal crown has been placed;

9 and let the robe and the horse be handed over to one of the king's most noble princes and let them array the man whom the king desires to honor and lead him on horseback through the city square, and proclaim before him, 'Thus it shall be done to the man whom the king desires to honor.'"

10 Then the king said to Haman, "Take quickly the robes and the horse as you have said, and do so for Mordecai the Jew, who is sitting at the king's gate; do not fall short in anything of all that you have said."

11 So Haman took the robe and the horse, and arrayed Mordecai, and led him on horseback through the city square, and proclaimed before him, "Thus it shall be done to the man whom the king desires to honor."

12 Then Mordecai returned to the king's gate. But Haman hurried home, mourning, with his head covered.

13 Haman recounted to Zeresh his wife and all his friends everything that had happened to him. Then his wise men and Zeresh his wife said to him, "If Mordecai, before whom you have begun to fall, is of Jewish origin, you will not overcome him, but will surely fall before him."

14 While they were still talking with him, the king's eunuchs arrived and hastily brought Haman to the banquet which Esther had prepared.

Chapter 7

1 Now the king and Haman came to drink wine with Esther the queen.

2 And the king said to Esther on the second day also as they drank their wine at the banquet, "What is your petition, Queen Esther? It shall be granted you. And what is your request? Even to half of the kingdom it shall be done."

3 Then Queen Esther replied, "If I have found favor in your sight, O king, and if it pleases the king, let my life be given me as my petition, and my people as my request;

4 for we have been sold, I and my people, to be destroyed, to be killed and to be annihilated. Now if we had only been sold as slaves, men and women, I would have remained silent, for the trouble would not be commensurate with the annoyance to the king."

5 Then King Ahasuerus asked Queen Esther, "Who is he, and where is he, who would presume to do thus?"

6 Esther said, "A foe and an enemy is this wicked Haman!" Then Haman became terrified before the king and queen.

7 The king arose in his anger from drinking wine and went into the palace garden; but Haman stayed to beg for his life from Queen Esther, for he saw that harm had been determined against him by the king.

8 Now when the king returned from the palace garden into the place where they were drinking wine, Haman was falling on the couch where Esther was. Then the king said, "Will he even assault the queen with

me in the house?" As the word went out of the king's mouth, they covered Haman's face.

9 Then Harbonah, one of the eunuchs who were before the king said, "Behold indeed, the gallows standing at Haman's house fifty cubits high, which Haman made for Mordecai who spoke good on behalf of the king!" And the king said, "Hang him on it."

10 So they hanged Haman on the gallows which he had prepared for Mordecai, and the king's anger subsided.

Chapter 8

1 On that day King Ahasuerus gave the house of Haman, the enemy of the Jews, to Queen Esther; and Mordecai came before the king, for Esther had disclosed what he was to her.

2 The king took off his signet ring which he had taken away from Haman, and gave it to Mordecai. And Esther set Mordecai over the house of Haman.

3 Then Esther spoke again to the king, fell at his feet, wept and implored him to avert the evil scheme of Haman the Agagite and his plot which he had devised against the Jews.

4 The king extended the golden scepter to Esther. So Esther arose and stood before the king.

5 Then she said, "If it pleases the king and if I have found favor before him and the matter seems proper to the king and I am pleasing in his sight, let it be written to revoke the letters devised by Haman, the son of Hammedatha the Agagite, which he wrote to destroy the Jews who are in all the king's provinces.

6 "For how can I endure to see the calamity which will befall my people, and how can I endure to see the destruction of my kindred?"

7 So King Ahasuerus said to Queen Esther and to Mordecai the Jew, "Behold, I have given the house of Haman to Esther, and him they have hanged on the gallows because he had stretched out his hands against the Jews.

8 "Now you write to the Jews as you see fit, in the king's name, and seal it with the king's signet ring; for a decree which is written in the name of the king and sealed with the king's signet ring may not be revoked."

9 So the king's scribes were called at that time in the third month (that is, the month Sivan), on the twenty-third day; and it was written according to all that Mordecai commanded to the Jews, the satraps, the governors and the princes of the provinces which extended from India to Ethiopia, 127 provinces, to every province according to its script, and to every people according to their language as well as to the Jews according to their script and their language.

10 He wrote in the name of King Ahasuerus, and sealed it with the king's signet ring, and sent letters by couriers on horses, riding on steeds sired by the royal stud.

11 In them the king granted the Jews who were in each and every city the right to assemble and to defend their lives, to destroy, to kill and to annihilate the entire army of any people or province which might attack them, including children and women, and to plunder their spoil,

12 on one day in all the provinces of King Ahasuerus, the thirteenth day of the twelfth month (that is, the month Adar).

13 A copy of the edict to be issued as law in each and every province was published to all the peoples, so that the Jews would be ready for this day to avenge themselves on their enemies.

14 The couriers, hastened and impelled by the king's command, went out, riding on the royal steeds; and the decree was given out at the citadel in Susa.

15 Then Mordecai went out from the presence of the king in royal robes of blue and white, with a large crown of gold and a garment of fine linen and purple; and the city of Susa shouted and rejoiced.

16 For the Jews there was light and gladness and joy and honor.

17 In each and every province and in each and every city, wherever the king's commandment and his decree arrived, there was gladness

and joy for the Jews, a feast and a holiday. And many among the peoples of the land became Jews, for the dread of the Jews had fallen on them.

Chapter 9

1 Now in the twelfth month (that is, the month Adar), on the thirteenth day when the king's command and edict were about to be executed, on the day when the enemies of the Jews hoped to gain the mastery over them, it was turned to the contrary so that the Jews themselves gained the mastery over those who hated them.

2 The Jews assembled in their cities throughout all the provinces of King Ahasuerus to lay hands on those who sought their harm; and no one could stand before them, for the dread of them had fallen on all the peoples.

3 Even all the princes of the provinces, the satraps, the governors and those who were doing the king's business assisted the Jews, because the dread of Mordecai had fallen on them.

4 Indeed, Mordecai was great in the king's house, and his fame spread throughout all the provinces; for the man Mordecai became greater and greater.

5 Thus the Jews struck all their enemies with the sword, killing and destroying; and they did what they pleased to those who hated them.

6 At the citadel in Susa the Jews killed and destroyed five hundred men,

7 and Parshandatha, Dalphon, Aspatha,

8 Poratha, Adalia, Aridatha,

9 Parmashta, Arisai, Aridai and Vaizatha,

10 the ten sons of Haman the son of Hammedatha, the Jews' enemy; but they did not lay their hands on the plunder.

11 On that day the number of those who were killed at the citadel in Susa was reported to the king.

12 The king said to Queen Esther, "The Jews have killed and destroyed

five hundred men and the ten sons of Haman at the citadel in Susa. What then have they done in the rest of the king's provinces! Now what is your petition? It shall even be granted you. And what is your further request? It shall also be done."

13 Then said Esther, "If it pleases the king, let tomorrow also be granted to the Jews who are in Susa to do according to the edict of today; and let Haman's ten sons be hanged on the gallows."

14 So the king commanded that it should be done so; and an edict was issued in Susa, and Haman's ten sons were hanged.

15 The Jews who were in Susa assembled also on the fourteenth day of the month Adar and killed three hundred men in Susa, but they did not lay their hands on the plunder.

16 Now the rest of the Jews who were in the king's provinces assembled, to defend their lives and rid themselves of their enemies, and kill 75,000 of those who hated them; but they did not lay their hands on the plunder.

17 This was done on the thirteenth day of the month Adar, and on the fourteenth day they rested and made it a day of feasting and rejoicing.

18 But the Jews who were in Susa assembled on the thirteenth and the fourteenth of the same month, and they rested on the fifteenth day and made it a day of feasting and rejoicing.

19 Therefore the Jews of the rural areas, who live in the rural towns, make the fourteenth day of the month Adar a holiday for rejoicing and feasting and sending portions of food to one another.

20 Then Mordecai recorded these events, and he sent letters to all the Jews who were in all the provinces of King Ahasuerus, both near and far,

21 obliging them to celebrate the fourteenth day of the month Adar, and the fifteenth day of the same month, annually,

22 because on those days the Jews rid themselves of their enemies, and it was a month which was turned for them from sorrow into gladness and from mourning into a holiday; that they should make them days

of feasting and rejoicing and sending portions of food to one another and gifts to the poor.

23 Thus the Jews undertook what they had started to do, and what Mordecai had written to them.

24 For Haman the son of Hammedatha, the Agagite, the adversary of all the Jews, had schemed against the Jews to destroy them and had cast Pur, that is the lot, to disturb them and destroy them.

25 But when it came to the king's attention, he commanded by letter that his wicked scheme which he had devised against the Jews, should return on his own head and that he and his sons should be hanged on the gallows.

26 Therefore they called these days Purim after the name of Pur. And because of the instructions in this letter, both what they had seen in this regard and what had happened to them,

27 the Jews established and made a custom for themselves and for their descendants and for all those who allied themselves with them, so that they would not fail to celebrate these two days according to their regulation and according to their appointed time annually.

28 So these days were to be remembered and celebrated throughout every generation, every family, every province and every city; and these days of Purim were not to fail from among the Jews, or their memory fade from their descendants.

29 Then Queen Esther, daughter of Abihail, with Mordecai the Jew, wrote with full authority to confirm this second letter about Purim.

30 He sent letters to all the Jews, to the 127 provinces of the kingdom of Ahasuerus, namely, words of peace and truth,

31 to establish these days of Purim at their appointed times, just as Mordecai the Jew and Queen Esther had established for them, and just as they had established for themselves and for their descendants with instructions for their times of fasting and their lamentations.

32 The command of Esther established these customs for Purim, and it was written in the book.

Chapter 10

1 Now King Ahasuerus laid a tribute on the land and on the coastlands of the sea.

2 And all the accomplishments of his authority and strength, and the full account of the greatness of Mordecai to which the king advanced him, are they not written in the Book of the Chronicles of the Kings of Media and Persia?

3 For Mordecai the Jew was second only to King Ahasuerus, and great among the Jews and in favor with his many kinsmen, one who sought the good of his people and one who spoke for the welfare of his whole nation.